This is an important and timely  attitudes to self-esteem traced h. then critiqued from the viewpoint of the Christian gospel. For me, one of the most valuable benefits has been to see how a human-centred cultural trend has crept unnoticed into the church. This has been a salutary warning to me personally. The book deserves to be widely read, both by thinking Christians and also by those outside the Christian church who want a fresh insight into the counter-cultural surprise of the gospel of grace. I commend it warmly.
Christopher Ash, Director of the Proclamation Trust's Cornhill Training Course

When I read the introduction to this book, I thought I might like it. I don't – I *love* it. It is high time that the urban myth of self-esteem was seriously questioned and intelligently trashed. This book does that and more. The reader gains a well-researched, thorough analysis of the love-yourself ideology, and of its impact on culture and (sadly) the church. But the second half of the book answers the questions raised by this malignant theology both theologically and practically.

Brilliant biblical uncommon sense for parents, youth workers, teachers, pastors and students of psychology everywhere.
Ann Benton, psychology graduate, teacher, speaker and writer on family issues

Parents, clergy, teachers and youth leaders need to read this book. It is scientifically authoritative but accessibly written, full of wit and engaging illustrations and stories (which I will certainly be 'borrowing' for sermons). Glynn debunks the myth that increasing self-esteem is the answer to all our problems, and replaces it with a much more real and true-to-life approach which takes account of our brokenness and failures, without losing sight of our preciousness to God. It therefore has the potential to reshape pastoral care and discipleship in a more biblical and genuinely supportive and life-changing way.
Revd Dr Sean Doherty, Tutor in Ethics, St Paul's Theological Centre, Holy Trinity Brompton, London

Professor Glynn Harrison is a psychiatrist with an engaging sense of self-deprecating humour and the ability to explain complex psychological theories with a felicitous lucidity. In *The Big Ego Trip* he stands in the tradition of Hans Christian Andersen in showing that the new psychology's emperor, aptly named 'Boosterism', in reality has no clothes on. At the same time, Dr Harrison displays compassion for, and offers hope to, those with deep psychological wounds (self-inflicted or otherwise). *The Big Ego Trip* is a 'must-read' not only for those with a special interest in psychology and psychiatry, but for all parents, teenagers and students – indeed for anyone seeking a trustworthy guide through the labyrinthine quest for self-esteem.

Sinclair B. Ferguson, Professor of Systematic Theology, Redeemer Theological Seminary, Dallas, Texas, USA

This thoroughgoing critique of the self-esteem movement provides insightful analysis of the conceptual muddle and cultural deficit it has generated. As the sweep of biblical teaching is applied to the central issues of our identity in a fresh and contemporary way, we are pointed consistently to the grace of God as the only source of Christian recovery and resilience, not just as a theory, but by many practical examples. Here is bedrock biblical sanity for a confused and crumbling culture, and a 'must-read' for every thoughtful Christian.

David Jackman, Past President of the Proclamation Trust

The apostle Paul challenged early followers of Jesus, 'Do not be conformed to this world, but be transformed by the renewal of your mind.' This exhortation is still timely and essential. We will either be shaped by the culture surrounding us or we will be shaped by God's Word. Glynn Harrison does an excellent job of identifying, analysing and critiquing the history and enormous influence of the self-esteem movement. He then develops a Christian approach to self that is biblical, intelligent and sensible. This book is fascinating, insightful and wise, and a wonderful resource to any Christian who wants to be 'transformed by the renewal of your mind'.

Dr Greg Pritchard, Director of European Leadership Forum and President of Communication Institute, Lisle, Illinois, USA

We have all felt the disappointment and pain which flow from living for self. This book compassionately invites us to enjoy God's healing power as we enjoy living for God and others.
Revd Dr Peter Sanlon, Curate, St Ann's, Tottenham

The Big Ego Trip is readily accessible and is written for a thinking Christian readership; it will be uniquely helpful to those working as psychotherapist, counsellor, health or social work professionals dealing with people, or to any helpful human being in every church. As a psychiatrist, the dilemma of self-esteem has troubled me for more than forty years: I know from my everyday practice that people are crippled by low self-esteem, but what I have learnt as a Christian directs me to deny myself and put others first – 'to be crucified with Christ'. How does one reconcile these apparently conflicting ideas?

In resolving this question, Glynn Harrison's unerring instinct for creative controversy has led him to a topic where he now makes a hugely insightful contribution. This book truly shows us the 'big picture', and I will strongly recommend it.

We are led on an intriguing stroll through the attractive but sinister byways of narcissism, the concept that we are 'worthy of happiness', 'boosterism' (feeling good about myself), and children treated as little princesses. All of this is contrasted with the very positive remedy of 'amazing grace'. We are recommended to stop judging ourselves, to be compassionate towards ourselves, but not to fall into the trap of a vacuous pursuit of self-esteem. This is a book to stimulate, and not stifle, debate amongst Christians on a topic that is of extreme relevance, but rarely mentioned in contemporary society.
Andrew Sims, Emeritus Professor of Psychiatry, University of Leeds; past President, Royal College of Psychiatrists

This is a timely and brilliant book on a neglected topic that goes to the heart of our cultural assumptions. Written with academic rigour, clinical compassion, incisive argument and biblical wisdom, delivered with a lightness of touch and self-deprecating humour.
Helen Willcox, Christian counsellor and psychotherapist

Glynn Harrison uses his vast experience in psychiatric practice and research to examine the cultural and psychological roots of the incredibly influential self-esteem movement. He summarizes, digests and evaluates huge amounts of research, and explains what he is doing with humour and many helpful examples, thus making complex ideas accessible to anyone. His conclusions are startling and have big consequences for education, psychology and counselling. In the last third of the book he builds an alternative foundation, from a Christian and biblical worldview, for how we should view ourselves, and thus demonstrates the profound practical implications of this new perspective for our lives and relationships. This is a superb example of a sharp Christian mind at work, helping us to evaluate the ways in which we have been seduced and brainwashed by our culture.

Richard Winter, psychotherapist and Professor of Practical Theology and Counseling, Covenant Theological Seminary, St Louis, Missouri, USA

THE BIG EGO TRIP

Finding true significance
in a culture of self-esteem

GLYNN HARRISON

INTER-VARSITY PRESS
Norton Street, Nottingham NG7 3HR England
Email: ivp@ivpbooks.com
Website: www.ivpbooks.com

First published 2013

British Library Cataloguing in Publication Data
A catalogue record for this book is available from the British Library.

ISBN: 978–1–84474–620–0

Set in Dante 12/15pt
Typeset in Great Britain by CRB Associates, Potterhanworth, Lincolnshire
Printed in Great Britain by Ashford Colour Press Ltd, Gosport, Hampshire

*Inter-Varsity Press publishes Christian books that are true to the Bible and that
communicate the gospel, develop discipleship and strengthen the church for its
mission in the world.*

*Inter-Varsity Press is closely linked with the Universities and Colleges Christian
Fellowship, a student movement connecting Christian Unions in universities and
colleges throughout Great Britain, and a member movement of the International
Fellowship of Evangelical Students. Website: www.uccf.org.uk*

For Amy, who labours on an island far away,
a guest of a greater reality . . .

CONTENTS

PREFACE

Why are there so many unsatisfactory books out there on self-esteem, I wondered? Now I know.

Self-esteem is a slippery concept that means so many different things to so many different people that it's impossible even to begin to meet expectations. It impacts upon a huge range of disciplines – psychology, psychiatry, biology, sociology, education, social policy, philosophy, theology – each with a contentious literature that stretches back decades, if not centuries, and leaves more questions than answers. So where do we begin? And when do we stop? Inevitably, this slim volume simply reflects where I've got to so far. I can only hope that, at the very least, it gets you thinking creatively about this topic.

I'm hugely grateful to so many individuals who have challenged and informed my thinking over the years. Monty Barker, a fellow psychiatrist, has been an inspiration and a model for nearly forty years. I'm grateful to other Christian-psychiatrist colleagues such as Richard Winter and Jan Truscott and, more recently, to Jon Haynes and Ben Watson.

In writing this book I owe a debt of gratitude to Ed Shaw for his advice and feedback on earlier drafts, and similarly to Christopher Ash for his encouragement and wisdom, and for his attempts to keep me on the theological straight and narrow. I doubt that he succeeded, however, and the many shortcomings are thus entirely mine. I'm grateful too to my editor Eleanor Trotter who has sustained my enthusiasm and offered crucial comments at just the right moments.

My daughters Rebecca, Amy and Abi have been a huge encouragement. Thank you. I need to thank Amy in particular for the hours spent diligently sorting out references, grammar and typos, and offering me really helpful feedback on the text. Most of all, I want to thank my wife Louise for her constant support, love and wisdom. Looking back over nearly forty years, she has certainly been good for my self-esteem, but I fear that sometimes I have been less than helpful to hers.

I've used many stories about various individuals throughout the book. I think it would be best to characterize them as 'inspired' by real events rather than faithful renditions. The stories all begin with real events, but in order to protect identities I've radically altered the details and even strung different stories together. So if you think the story is about you, well . . . it's not. Which takes me to the theme of the book: Life isn't about you!

In the light of God's big picture, an over-arching story vastly superior to our small worlds, how should we think about ourselves? I hope and pray that this important question will help you to get started.

Glynn Harrison
Bristol, 2012

INTRODUCTION

Show me someone without an ego and I'll show you a loser.
Donald Trump[1]

In a large theatre in Seattle, USA an overweight young mobile phone salesman called Stuart steps up to the microphone to audition for a TV talent show. His gait, bearing, facial expression – the whole body-language package – signals that here, ladies and gentlemen, we have a loser.

Stuart is going to sing 'opera'. As the judges glance sideways and roll their eyes, the audience sit back and wait for the fun to begin. What follows is a spine-tingling, lump-in-the-throat rendition of 'Nessun Dorma' that brings the audience to its feet and the judges to their knees. It's an electrifying piece of theatre that lays the foundations for huge recording contracts and international stardom.

But our young performer discovers another kind of stardom too. Within no time at all his story finds its way into inspirational seminars, life-changing coaching programmes and onto websites that promise to revolutionize your life. It turns out that, like Stuart, you too can release your inner strength, find your power and discover your destiny. Only 'believe in yourself . . .'

In a London inner-city school, an eight-year-old schoolgirl sits enthralled. A teacher is telling the story of 'mouse'. 'Poor mouse,' says the teacher. 'She's forgotten that she has her own special gift. "I'm no good; I'm only a mouse!"'

'Believe in yourself,' the little girl whispers.

'I'm no good; I'm only a mouse!'

'Believe in yourself,' her classmates join in. 'Believe in yourself.' As the children try to convince mouse that it's 'good' to be who she is, it's repeated over and over: 'Believe in yourself!'

At the end of the lesson the children file out of the assembly room, chanting, 'It's good to be me, good to be me.' A school inspector sitting towards the rear of the classroom nods his quiet approval: a whole-school self-esteem policy that works.

In New York a black American pop singer is being interviewed for the latest issue of *Hello!* magazine. Described as a 'global phenomenon', she offers the usual briefing about her taste in fashion, boyfriends and the inevitable plug for her latest record. Then comes an unexpected question. The interviewer asks her to confide her 'greatest sin'.

After a few moments of reflection, with utter sincerity she makes her confession. 'My greatest sin . . .' she intones, 'is that I've never truly loved myself.'

In a nearby courtroom a young woman stands impassively as she waits for the verdict. 'Guilty,' announces the spokesperson for the jury. A roar of approval erupts from the gallery. The hardened, pasty face of a mother who had cruelly abused and neglected her baby son contorts in fear and perplexity. 'What's going to happen to me now?' she screams to the judge. 'The defendant has low intelligence,' her counsel pleads in mitigation, 'and, coming from an abusive family herself, she suffers with chronically low self-esteem.' Before sentencing, the judge calls for full social and psychological reports.

In Bristol, England a group of five-year-olds at a birthday party sit restlessly in a small circle, one of them clutching a large brown parcel. As music from the 'Teddy Bears' Picnic' strikes up, the precious parcel begins to move erratically from hand to hand. It's 'pass the parcel'. Suddenly the music stops, and wide-eyed Alice left holding the parcel rips off a layer of wrapping to claim a chocolate prize. The music starts again and the pattern continues, each 'spontaneous' pause allowing another child to claim a small prize. Mysteriously, by the end of the game, each child clutches a similarly sized bar of chocolate. 'You can't have losers,' winks the mother in charge of the music. 'Not good for their self-esteem!'

In a small church hall in the Midwest of the United States a young mother is calling her Sunday school class to order. A wall poster displays a fair-skinned Jesus, smiling benignly at a group of Western children gathered around his knee.

'You're special!' he is telling them.

'Today,' the teacher announces, 'we are going to let off a little *self-esteam!*' None of the kids gets the joke.

The world of self-esteem

Welcome to the world of self-esteem. Half a century ago if somebody complained of feeling down or felt that nobody liked them, that they were 'no good' or that they didn't like themselves, a friend would most likely offer advice along the following lines:

'Don't get stuck in your own problems. Don't think about yourself so much. Instead of being a "here-I-am" sort of person, try to be a "there-you-are" person! Think about other people. Try to get out more. Make new friends and explore some new interests. You'll never get anywhere by contemplating your own navel.'

Today the same friend would offer this same person radically different counsel:

'You need to believe in yourself more! Stop thinking so much about other people's problems and worrying about other people's expectations. You need to discover who you are. Be yourself. Learn to like yourself. Build up your self-esteem.'

How life has changed, and not just in the counselling room or on the psychiatrist's couch. The stories above (with details changed, but all rooted in real events) show just how far the self-esteem idea has penetrated Western culture. Everybody is 'special' and we must all receive prizes. Because psychologists tell us that 'low self-esteem' seeds educational failure and mental illness, we try to inoculate our kids from their very earliest years: 'You're incredible!'; 'Danger, princess on board!'; 'What have we here, a Mozart in the making or what?!' And when they grow up into mature adults striving for success and recognition, the message just keeps on coming: 'You just need to believe in yourself!'

Things have changed in our churches too. I sat in a committee meeting recently, addressed by a chirpy young 'church-growth consultant' sporting a spiky haircut and a PowerPoint presentation. Clicking on yet another depressing graph showing national church attendance figures heading southwards, he announced, 'Our churches need leaders who will help them build up their self-esteem.'

In my Sunday school days many decades ago we sang a little song that went, 'Jesus first, myself last, and others in between . . . ' We would never teach our children to sing such self-negating tunes now. Why not? 'Because you can't love other people until first you love yourself.' In this upside-down world of self-esteem it's not the sin of pride that we take into the confessional, but the transgression of 'not liking myself enough'.

Hardly anybody disagrees with this now. It's a no-brainer. Self-esteem ideology has gained acceptance among lawyers and academics, as well as politicians, educationalists and church leaders. In academic psychology it's one of the most published topics in the whole of the psychological literature. What happened to bring this about? And how did the self-esteem movement gain such a foothold in our lives?

The big fix

First, the self-esteem idea promised big. What started out with good intentions – to help a minority crushed by criticism to stop beating themselves up and take a more realistic view – became a one-size-fits-all solution needed by everybody. This didn't just apply to bad feelings linked with a difficult and emotionally toxic childhood either. Self-esteem ideology made a land grab for the big questions of significance and personal 'value' too.

Everybody has questions about their value and significance. Since the beginning of time humans have puzzled over questions of where we figure in the grand scheme of things and what we are 'worth'. The ancients asked, 'What is man that you are mindful of him, the son of man that you care for him?' (Psalm 8:4). The prophets of the Old Testament told us to 'stop trusting in man, who has but a breath in his nostrils. Of what account is he?' (Isaiah 2:22). And Eastern sages lamented, 'Meaningless! Meaningless! . . . Utterly meaningless! Everything is meaningless' (Ecclesiastes 1:2).

Even now, in the Higgs-boson era, issues of significance continue to haunt us. As I write this, for example, I notice an uneasy feeling growing in a corner of my mind. What, I wonder, will you, the reader, think of what I am saying? And by extension, what will you think of *me*? How will this book affect the way I'm perceived, the attention that I'm awarded and the recognition that I crave? I find myself looking to you, the reader, to resolve the question of my significance. The self-esteem movement gripped our imagination because it engaged with this, the deepest and most profound problem of our lives – the struggle for significance and self-worth – and it told us it could fix it.

Secondly, the self-esteem idea had experts. Oh yes, massed ranks of them. And the experts told us that efforts to promote self-worth (or 'boosterism' as I prefer to call it[2]) work. This was science after all. They convinced us that there was enough objective, scientific evidence about the terrible toll that low self-esteem wreaks in our lives to merit radical and far-reaching changes to the way we think about ourselves. They said that, because bad self-esteem is learned, it can be unlearned – provided we recruit enough parents, teachers, Sunday school leaders and counsellors to the cause. Soon, in response to their clarion call, a vast army of self-help gurus, educationalists and 'cultural entrepreneurs' stood ready to fill the breach.

Thirdly, when the self-esteem movement took off nearly half a century ago, it resonated perfectly with the emerging spirit of the age. After surfing the sexual revolution of the 1960s, self-esteem ideology thrived in the new humanisms of the 1970s and the materialistic orgies of the 1980s. Eventually, the primacy of self-admiration became the default cultural mode: If we want to love one another, first we have to learn to love ourselves – right? Who could disagree with that? And hey, hadn't Jesus even said something about loving your neighbour *as yourself*? We overdosed on self-admiration, and, as a result, the self-esteem movement gained a powerful foothold in the Western mind, and reshaped secular and Christian cultures alike.

The big con?

But did it work? It was only after decades of promoting self-esteem that academic psychologists got around to asking this, the most important question of all. Had it delivered on its promises? Did encouraging people to value, love and honour themselves produce the kind of outcomes we had all hoped for? Exactly where was the hard evidence?

The methodology used to answer these questions was rigorous and statistically complex, but what they discovered was relatively simple and straightforward. It hadn't delivered and it didn't work. Their reviews showed there was little evidence that boosterism produced any of the benefits claimed: no positive findings were uncovered in the field of education; negative results stacked up in the area of mental health; and there was nothing to write home about in the fields of social adjustment and healthy relationships.

More worryingly, psychologists began to lay the blame for a whole raft of unhappy social trends – the rise of celebrity culture, a preoccupation with rights and entitlement, the growth of selfishness and narcissism – at the door of the self-esteem movement. It turned out that the doctrine of self-esteem had promised big but delivered small.

The big ego trip

I am going to attempt to convince you that self-esteem is a failed ideology. I will argue that the 'science' is based on a statistical fallacy, that there is little evidence that efforts to promote self-esteem work, and that, in its popular form of 'boosterism', self-esteem promotion comes with hazardous and unwanted side effects.

Of course a rounded and realistic view of ourselves is a

necessary and important component of healthy psychological development. I am not arguing against the need for an accurate self-concept. So in this book we are going to explore the need for what I call 'radical self-compassion'. But questions of *value* and *self-worth* need to be sorted out in the context of a larger 'story' about our identity and purpose. We need a wholly different approach to the age-old question of how we should think about ourselves than the simplistic tenets of boosterism.

This is a book of two parts. We won't be ready to discard self-esteem ideology until and unless we are fully convinced of its failure. Self-esteem's vice-like grip on popular culture – on your heart and mind – is simply too strong. So in the first part of the book I am going to tell the story of how we came to believe that the riddle of human worth and significance, feelings of guilt and shame, inferiority and low confidence, could be solved by the 'science' of psychology and the merits of self-esteem. We will plot the steady ascent of the self-esteem idea, from a relatively simple insight by an American psychologist called William James in 1890 through its mutation into a modern-day meme, a self-replicating cultural unit that infected populations like a virus. It has been said that all ideas are 'egotists bent on world domination',[3] and I am going to try to convince you that self-esteem ideology belongs up there in the pantheon of the twentieth century's 'big ideas', meriting comparison with feminism and Freudianism. We shall explore how self-esteem ideology colonized the Western mind, penetrating the worlds of education, public health and religion with an influence way beyond the psychological evidence on which it was supposed to rest. For unless we understand the scale of this cultural change, we shall never find sufficient motivation to unpick its influence in our own hearts, or to rescue our children from its claim on their lives.

The bigger-than-your-ego trip

In the second part of this book I will ask whether there is a biblical and more psychologically secure approach to the big questions of significance and worth. The good news, I believe, is that there is. The bad news is that it comes in a form that is completely anathema to contemporary Western culture. It doesn't lend itself to quick fixes and it can't be marketed in advertising slogans. As hard as I try, it's impossible to get the word 'just' into it. It's definitely not achievable in sixty seconds, and it can't be squeezed into ten steps, five key strategies or even seven habits. In an era that wants instant fulfilment and expects everything to be effortless, I am definitely on the back foot here.

But if we want to know how we should think about ourselves, we must face up to the 'worldview' issues of identity and purpose. Who am I? And, more importantly, what am I *for*? Psychologists can't provide the answer to such ultimate questions. They can plunder insights from philosophy, neuroscience and literature, but these disciplines eventually send us back to the riddle that lies at the heart of the experience of every human being: How should we think about ourselves? Where do we figure in the big scheme of things? And why are we so hungry for significance?

Our answers to these questions pivot around the deeper questions of God and whether he has revealed himself to us. If there is no God, no truth revealed from beyond human imagination, then indeed we are on our own. Philosophically we must attempt to construct ourselves as best we can, 'make ourselves up' as we go along and use whatever materials lie to hand. From this perspective we can think about ourselves in just about any way we like. But my argument in this book is that those who opt to make 'self-worth' the core project of their lives can't rely upon the 'science' of psychology to validate their beliefs. Everything, you see, comes back to philosophy.

If there is a God, and if he has revealed himself in the Christian gospel, then we have a story to live by. And that changes everything. First, and perhaps most importantly of all, it changes our perspective or 'mindset'. Instead of aiming for 'what's good for me', we are called to aim for what's good for his kingdom and what's good for his glory. It's not about you! This is God's big story, and, as we remodel the plot-line of our lives around its beckoning destiny, we discover the liberation of self-forgetfulness. Like happiness, you see, true significance is discovered in aiming for something else.

Secondly, it changes our sense of identity. As Christians, we need to develop, and then psychologically 'inhabit', our story-shaped identity as loved children of God. We need to learn to 'think' like loved children of God, gradually reshaping the brokenness of the past around the promise of the future. Here is the context in which we can find how to stop judging and evaluating ourselves altogether, and instead adopt a biblical self-compassion. And here is the context in which we can learn to dispute and reject the consequences of the sin 'done to us', as well as discover forgiveness and grace for the sin committed by us.

True significance is discovered in aiming for something else.

This is no quick-fix. But if we stay the course, we will discover that, in contrast to the flattery offered by certain cosmetic companies, here is something that really is 'worth it'. Compared with the failed ideology of self-esteem, the gospel offers us the ultimate 'bigger-than-my-ego' trip. So let's strap ourselves in for the ride and start at the beginning. Today's obsession with self-esteem – how did it all begin?

1. BIRTH OF AN IDEOLOGY

On Saturday 22 November 2003, just twenty-six seconds before the end of the game, England bagged the Rugby World Cup with a last-gasp drop goal by Jonny Wilkinson. The crowd erupted, sworn enemies hugged in jubilation and grown men wept. A hero was born. Since first walking on to a rugby pitch as a youngster, here was everything the young Jonny Wilkinson had been working towards. It should have been the greatest moment of his life. And yet within hours he was 'tumbling out of control'.

What happened? In his book, *Tackling Life*,[1] Wilkinson tells how for years he was haunted by anxiety. Stalked by insecurity and self-doubt, life was like a game that he couldn't win. Instead he found himself chained to a treadmill of achievement in which you are only as good as your last kick. The better things were, the more he had to lose.

Many of us have experienced similar feelings. Like Jonny Wilkinson, we try to feel better by being better. And then, stuck on a treadmill of achievement and addicted to other people's approval, we just keep on running. So could this be a problem with 'self-esteem'? And could we learn to feel better about ourselves more generally by *thinking differently* about our goals, our achievements and our efforts?

The achievement game

The first person to coin the term 'self-esteem' was William James,[2] an American widely credited as the 'father of modern psychology'.[3] And, like Jonny Wilkinson, James linked the way we feel about ourselves to the way we think about our goals and achievements in life.

Born in 1842 to a well-to-do New York family,[4] young William was something of a polymath. His interests straddled the fields of philosophy, medicine and the emerging discipline of psychology. The family were all high achievers: William's father, Henry, was an exponent of the Swedish Christian mystic Emanuel Swedenborg; Henry Jr, William's brother, was a budding novelist. The family travelled widely and enjoyed a refined and cosmopolitan lifestyle.

But William battled with mental health problems and, despite graduating in medicine from Harvard, he never practised as a doctor. Instead he decided to take up psychology. A prolific writer and achiever, his works are a potent reminder that psychology was then only slowly emerging as a separate discipline from philosophy. In fact, James also founded the philosophical school of *pragmatism* and he is widely credited with inventing the term.

James was interested in the *feelings* generated when we evaluate or assess our achievements. In his view, the human mind prizes achievement above all else, and the more successful we are, the better we feel about ourselves generally. He taught that, if you take time to observe your thoughts and reflect on your attitudes, you soon realize that, like Wilkinson, you are an *evaluator*. We constantly score or 'rate' our achievements as a means of scoring and rating ourselves as whole people ('I'm a hopeless communicator, so I feel like a hopeless person'; 'I'm a great hockey player, one of the best, so that makes me a pretty awesome person').

As the scoring game gradually settles down into an overall pattern, James taught that this produces a more general 'self-feeling' or 'emotional tone of feeling'. In other words, although on any given day your feelings can go up and down, depending on how well the scores are going, over time they will merge to create an 'average tone of self-feeling' in an 'I-just-feel-hopeless-about-myself' sort of way or an 'I'm-a-living-legend' sort of way.

This doesn't apply to any old achievements, however. We have to be competent in areas that matter to us. If you've always wanted to be a football player, it's no use discovering that you are a great ballet dancer. Hence, James said, self-esteem depends on the ratio of our actual achievements compared to our expectations: our hopes, dreams and ambitions. The more our achievements line up with our dreams, the better we feel about ourselves.

This doesn't mean that self-esteem is set in concrete and can't be changed. James believed that, if you really want to, you can change your feelings by changing the way you think about your achievements. It's no use trying to feel good about yourself by looking in the mirror and telling yourself you are a wonderful, marvellous, loveable you. James didn't believe in boosterism. To change your feelings about yourself, he said, you either have to bring your achievements into closer line with your dreams or modify those dreams: what you're aiming for in life.

Take the example of our football-aspiring ballet dancer: you can either stick with your goal and work harder to achieve it ('I'm going to work at kicking this ball until my feet drop off'), or you can change your goal and the way you think about it ('Hey, ballet dancing is pretty cool after all and I don't care what other people think').

Either way, James opened the door to the possibility that self-esteem is something that we can change by focusing on the way we think about our goals and aspirations. So he would probably have advised somebody like Jonny Wilkinson to stop aiming for a perfect score, modify his ambitions and go for something more realistic. He would never have suggested that he should try to boost self-esteem by rehearsing statements such as 'You are special'. And he would have been shocked by the manner in which feeling good about yourself, regardless of your achievements, became the big 'must-have' of the later part of the twentieth century.

The ego game

With the dawn of the twentieth century, however, James' popularity began to wane under the growing influence of the Austrian neurologist and psychoanalyst, Sigmund Freud. Although Freud didn't actually use the term 'self-esteem', he had a great deal to say about how we come to adopt negative and positive attitudes and feelings towards ourselves. But instead of linking these self-feelings with our achievements in the 'here and now', Freud focused on their origins in early-infant development: the 'there and then'. In other words, if you want to help people who struggle like Jonny Wilkinson, you have to get them on the couch and back to their childhood roots. Freud taught that positive and negative feelings about ourselves depend crucially on what happens to us in early childhood. In particular, they pivot on the outcome of momentous struggles between different 'bits' of the personality that take place at that time. What did he mean?

Freud's model of the human mind is best pictured as three compartments: the id, the ego and the super-ego,[5] connected by tubes, with psychic forces flowing between them. Freud knew that these structures don't actually exist in the brain, but insisted that his model helps us to understand how the different operations of the mind relate to one another.

The id is the most primitive compartment and develops first. To understand the id, just take a look at how babies and infants operate: 'I want, I need, I must have, not tomorrow, not even in five minutes' time, but NOW.' The id is all about me. It has one simple operating principle, or rule, summed up in Freud's concept of the 'pleasure principle': to get its own satisfaction. Described as a 'dark inaccessible part of the personality',[6] the id is driven by raw aggression and irresistible surges of desire for sexual gratification.

The id wants to rule the world, and, if it could get its way, we would feel very good indeed about ourselves. But of course a world populated by unfettered ids would be a nightmare wasteland of rape, pillage and destruction. So the instincts and demands of the id need to be toned down, which is where our parents come in. When little Harry screams, 'I want, I need, I must have, not tomorrow, not even in five minutes' time, but NOW', his id hits the buffers of his parents' discipline. He discovers that the promised ice cream stays in the fridge and he is invited to spend five minutes on the naughty step.

So here we have the beginnings of feeling bad about ourselves. It is this experience of parental discipline that develops and builds Freud's second compartment of the mind, which he called the 'over-ego' or 'super-ego'. This is the place where little Harry absorbs the standards, ideals, expectations and rules of his parents. Over time, as he absorbs his parents' rules and strictures, he even comes to adopt them, as if they were his own idea in the first place. In other words, his super-ego takes over from where mum and dad left off and operates as its own 'moral policeman'. And, as we shall see, the super-ego is very good at making us feel bad about ourselves.

But surely the id, possessing the sheer brute force of its aggression and the intoxicating seduction of sex, wins out every time? Not so, because the super-ego has a secret weapon up its sleeve: the powerful, crushing emotion that we call *guilt*. If we dare to yield to the id, the super-ego tips a bucketful of self-condemnation right over our heads. The super-ego can make you feel *terrible* about yourself. And here, according to Freud, is the root of 'feeling bad about yourself'. Too much guilt, too much super-ego, and we grow up nursing an aching sense of negative self-feeling. Or, as we would say today, we grow up with low self-esteem.

Most of what I have described so far takes place at an unconscious level. The third compartment of the mind, however – the ego – is the conscious part. The ego sits between the id and the super-ego and acts as a kind of referee. As the ego tries to relate to the outside world, its task is to balance the 'inner beast' of the id against the moral sensitivities of the super-ego and come up with a working compromise. That's not easy of course, which is why, according to Freud, we often feel like a walking civil war.

The poor old ego. Why doesn't it simply get crushed under the weight of the guilt that the super-ego doles out? Well, the ego has a secret weapon of its own: the infant's natural tendency towards 'grandiosity' or, as Freud put it, his 'narcissism'. Infants are naturally grandiose, Freud said, tending to view other people purely as supply-lines for the needs of their id. So when the super-ego doles out a bucketful of guilt, the infant's natural grandiosity acts as a sort of buffer to lessen its impact and smooth things out. And then, with the passage of time, the ego moderates its narcissism into something more rounded, what Freud called 'positive self-regard'.

Good self-regard is a kind of protective mechanism. As they steer a steady course between the outrageous demands of the id and the punishing expectations of the super-ego, people with a healthy dose of positive self-regard hold their heads up high. In fact, over time, they even take the demands and expectations of the super-ego and reshape them into their own 'ego-ideals' or moral standards. And that makes them feel even better about themselves. And here we have the basis for what some later called 'good' self-esteem.

Let me give an example. Dad may look very angry indeed and tell us that, if we ever tell a lie like that again, we will miss our pudding and be grounded from using our computer for a whole week! Ouch. The super-ego takes the point, doles out a helping of guilt and condemnations, and we slink away with our tail between our legs. The message is clear: Don't tell lies because bad things happen when you do. Over time, however, the ego shapes the guilt-laden stricture: 'Don't tell lies or else . . . ', and turns it into something more positive, such as 'Be a person of integrity and self-respect, and that's how you will win friends and influence people.' And that makes us feel much better about ourselves.

So Freud's contribution to the idea of self-esteem was to suggest that, despite all the disgusting effluent spewing forth from the id, we develop a more positive moral view of ourselves by nurturing positive 'self-regard'. Decades later, when psychologists became interested in the concept of self-esteem, many drew on Freud's positive self-regard as their basic model. Here was the inspiration for the modern idea that 'thinking positively' or 'feeling good' about oneself is the key to defeating guilt and self-blame, overcoming low confidence, and finding significance and worth. Forgetting William James' emphasis on the way we think about our achievements in the here and now, the focus shifted to Freud's emphasis upon the past, and to the warfare that takes place within the personality. To this way of thinking, unless something is done, those exposed to overly harsh parental discipline, or who harbour unrealistic 'ego-ideals', seem doomed to low self-esteem forever.

The inferiority game

Freud had many disciples and his ground-breaking ideas spawned several different schools of psychoanalysis that took different directions. Alfred Adler (a fellow Austrian), for example, became increasingly interested in the way in which those power dynamics that Freud said operate within the personality (between the id and super-ego) also operate between people (not least between him and Freud!). In fact, Adler's interest in politics, and especially the power struggles in contemporary movements such as socialism and feminism, provoked him to develop much further Freud's interest in themes of power and control.[7]

It was Adler who coined the popular notion of the 'inferiority complex'. In the infant, he said, the adult's all-controlling power provokes a deep sense of inferiority. Simply put, adults are big and babies are small, and that makes us feel bad about ourselves. Those inferiority feelings have a positive function, however, because they goad the infant forwards towards mastery and success. It is a determination to 'join the adult club' and defeat inferiority that spurs the infant on in his thirst for knowledge, competence and wisdom. For Adler, the genius of early feelings of inferiority is that they motivate us to do and be our best.

But of course it doesn't work that way for everybody. Some children, landed with parents who undermine rather than nurture their fledgling confidence, get saddled with an 'inferiority complex'. And there's another twist to this sorry tale too. Some children over-reach themselves in the fight back and put on a false 'front' of superiority. The result is Adler's 'superiority complex', the bloated personality that shares many of the features of Freud's narcissist.

So Adler was another key foundational thinker for the self-esteem movement. His narratives of early-infant power struggles, and the resulting inferiority complex, fed directly into our modern assumption that negative self-feelings are rooted in early-infant experiences of harsh and humiliating parents. And his superiority complex paved the way for the idea of 'fragile self-esteem': a prideful, over-assertive and overbearing façade ('chip on the shoulder') that is supposed to mask a turmoil of inferiority lurking underneath.

The shrinking game

Just as contemporary power plays and rivalries helped to mould Adler's thought, personal struggles with power and domination sculpted the thinking of the psychoanalyst Karen Horney too. In her case, it was authoritarian men such as her father (and not least Freud himself) who provided the catalyst to her creative thought. And like William James, her frequent bouts of depression fuelled curiosity into the origins of her own feelings of inferiority.[8]

Horney was a Freudian at heart, so once again she takes us into the distant past of early childhood. Like Adler, she focused on the infant's sense of isolation and helplessness in a potentially hostile world. Horney was particularly interested in the way in which some parents' behaviour can lead a child to doubt her basic approval and acceptance. When this happens, Horney said, the child comes to perceive love and encouragement as 'contingent' or dependent. In other words, we only feel OK about ourselves when other people seem OK towards us. As a result, we grow up feeling insecure and react to the world with fearfulness or 'basic anxiety'.[9]

But, like Adler, Horney believed that the self fights back. The most common fight-back mechanism is what Horney called the *shrinking self*.[10] In this case, the infant surrenders before war can be declared, and waves the white flag of capitulation in the face of the slightest threat. Such children grow up to become adults with weak and insecure boundaries, living to satisfy other people's expectations. This is the sort of person who invites you to a gourmet feast for Sunday lunch by offering an apology for her cooking. The shrinking self is deeply insecure and dominated by worthlessness: a classic case of what we now call 'low self-esteem'.

The *expansive self*, on the other hand, says that you have to strike first. In other words, before war can be declared, the infant launches a pre-emptive strike. These children, said Horney, grow up to be dominating, know-it-all, 'conquest' personality types who need to control those around them. Here we have a picture of the tetchy and defensive shop-floor manager, bald and 5 ft 5 in tall, aggressively relishing the power he holds over other people's lives, or the kind of person for whom the smallest criticism launches an armada of self-justification. These are classic cases of what would later be called 'fragile self-esteem' or, in popular language, having a 'chip on your shoulder'.

Horney's unique insight was to spot the importance of consistent and non-contingent parental love that offers 'unconditional acceptance'. Where this is missing, we have another root of what would later be called low self-esteem.

The attachment game

Before we try to pull these different threads together, we need to look briefly at one more model of infant development. In the 1960s, shortly before the self-esteem movement really took off, 'attachment theory' burst onto the psychology scene. Attachment theory was the brainchild of the psychoanalyst and psychiatrist John Bowlby.[11]

For healthy psychological development and mature adult relationships, Bowlby also emphasized the need for a secure emotional bond with a primary caregiver, usually the mother, which allows the child to *attach* to her. This process, which occurs sometime between six and twenty-four months, plays a core role in the development of the infant's 'internal working model' for how to initiate and maintain healthy relationships later in life.

There are a number of very plausible ideas in Bowlby's work. It rings true that a secure relationship with the chief caregiver in early life sets the pace for how we approach relationships later in life. If a child experiences inconsistent affection and erratic care from his drug-addicted mother, we wouldn't be surprised if, as an adult, he himself has difficulty with commitment and in trusting other human beings to behave faithfully. Bowlby's ideas have been subjected to a fair degree of empirical testing too, with carers and children being observed under experimental conditions.[12] So attachment theory has some important things to say about how we develop our concept of ourselves.

Bowlby was more or less ostracized from the psychoanalytic community for betraying some of its most fundamental tenets, but his attachment theory gained considerable status and academic recognition. Among professionals operating in child welfare services, it is probably now one of the most popular theories for explaining difficulties in parent-child relationships.[13]

The self-esteem movement was also deeply influenced by Bowlby's work. Although Bowlby himself held self-esteem ideology in contempt for its simplistic reductionism, that didn't prevent the movement from hijacking his insights. According to its theorists, malformed attachment was just another cause of low self-esteem.

It's all in the mind, stupid!

So how do we draw these threads together? We have considered just a few snippets from a handful of theorists and counsellors. Academics will wince at the speed and superficiality of this brief survey of some of the greatest thinkers of the last century. But the ideas I have chosen are those that were in the main used as building blocks for the development of self-esteem theory in the mid-twentieth century. In this brief overview I have simply attempted to trace the key streams of thought that in the late 1960s eventually converged into the powerful river of self-esteem. This involved three key developments.

First, at popular level, these different and complex theories about the development of early-infant personality were condensed into one simple concept of low self-worth. Whether it was the psychoanalysts' work on positive and negative self-regard, Adler's inferiority complex or Horney's shrinking personality, these imaginative and far-reaching ideas were essentially collapsed into the economical concept of low self-esteem. This also had the added advantage of producing something relatively straightforward and easy to grasp.

Secondly, low self-esteem came to be seen as a condition that affects almost everybody. Theories that had been constructed around the harrowing and damaged narratives of a few (and that remain immensely helpful for some) were generalized to the many. Low self-esteem came to be seen as everybody's problem and then linked with a wide range of psychological and social issues. And so, thirdly, as a result, 'boosterism' was born. If low self-esteem formed in early life is the problem, then boosting self-esteem must be the solution. Thus the idea was born that everybody, everywhere, will benefit from a liberal dose of self-admiration. Especially people like Jonny Wilkinson . . .

But what was it about the concept of self-esteem that allowed it to take off so spectacularly? How come it has been so successful? What happened in the 1960s that turned this simplistic piece of popular reductionism into a movement, and then turned a movement into a way of life?

2. TIPPING POINT

It takes just one more thing. A small tremor of the hand, a slight nudge against the elbow, the very last card eased into place, and the whole house comes toppling down. You have reached a 'tipping point', the simple physics-based principle that a small amount of weight added to a finely balanced object can cause it abruptly and completely to collapse.

It's the same with people's behaviour. Back in the late 1950s a sociologist called Morton Grodzins was studying patterns of racism in American neighbourhoods.[1] He discovered that white families stayed in a neighbourhood as long as the number of black families remained comparatively small. But at some point the 'one-too-many' moment arrives and the remaining white families exit en masse. This is the moment he called the tipping point.

We can think about the spread of ideas in the same way. How come some ideas get to turn themselves into self-evident truths that take over the whole world, while others languish in obscurity? Why do some ideas catch on? It's because they reach a tipping point, a 'moment of critical mass, the threshold, the boiling point',[2] when a set of favourable conditions merges to give lift-off. The new idea spreads like a viral epidemic and, once embedded, even in the face of evidence to the contrary, becomes so culturally acceptable that we just *want* to believe it. Like alcohol, when an idea has colonized our minds it can numb our critical faculty to the point that we just want more.

The march of science

But scientific ideas do not progress like this, do they? In the world of science it's the quality of the evidence, surely, which determines how far up the food chain an idea manages to crawl?

We like to think that *scientific* facts sit neatly in rows patiently waiting to be observed. The process of discovery, we believe, is overseen by a scientific community dedicated to truth and objectivity and guided by the strict codes of the scientific method. Its members diligently test and probe, sift and search, discard the useless and preserve the good. In contrast to the cynical old hacks who dominate the media and the foul-mouthed spin doctors who control politics, scientific knowledge producers can be trusted to tell it how it is. They are the objective cartographers of nature's vast landscape and the faithful stewards of her hidden secrets.

This basic trust of science isn't confined to physics and chemistry. We have baptized the newer sciences of sociology and psychology with the same reverence and respect. We believe that the methods which produced startling benefits in the fields of transport and manufacturing can be released to create similar wonders in our understanding of society, relationships and the human mind. And we hope that, in these areas too, science manages to stand aloof from the vagaries

of fashion and the power structures that control the development of 'ordinary' ideas.

But it doesn't work like that. True, under strictly controlled
conditions, *individual* scientific facts can be subjected to careful
scrutiny, and then sifted and tested with a considerable degree
of objectivity. But in complex areas such as the study of
human behaviour, individual facts have to be merged to create
bigger facts, or stories, about reality. And this is where the
problems begin, because social and emotional factors that
arbitrate the progress of other ideas come into play here as
well. And as a result, some scientific ideas become powerful
and widespread, while others have to settle for remaining
weak and local.[3]

Don't misunderstand me. I am not buying into a post-
modernist rejection of the scientific method as 'just another
way of knowing'. I don't think that we 'just have to choose
what to believe', depending on the goodness of fit with the
language culture of our local community. The scientific
method has produced extraordinary goods for humankind. But
the discoveries of science need to be tested and retested and
then tested again, before they can achieve the status of facts.

Once a new fact has broken through into popular culture,
however, it can sometimes assume a life of its own, even when
there has been a severe weakening of the objective scientific
evidence behind it. Only the other day somebody reminded
me that 'of course, we only use 10% of our brains, don't we?'
When I give talks on psychiatry and brain science, this kind
of thing comes up all the time. It pops up in newspapers and
popular magazines too. But there is no evidence that the 10%
'fact' is true.[4] If somebody gets a bullet in the head, you don't
hear a brain surgeon reassuring us that 'luckily it passed
through the 90% of the brain that doesn't get used'. The
notion that we only use 10% of our brains is a classic urban

legend. So why does it persist? Simply because, in terms of the untapped potential it could release, it would be so nice if it were true. Like so many uplifting myths, the truth of the matter seems to be its least important aspect.

Something similar to this happened in the late 1960s and the 1970s when self-esteem ideology exploded into popular culture. Self-esteem reached its cultural tipping point. So what were the factors behind its success?

Academic lift-off

Self-esteem's cultural tipping point came on the back of spectacular success in the academic sphere. As we saw earlier, after William James the term 'self-esteem' remained dormant and largely unnoticed for nearly half a century. Then, in the late 1960s, it broke through academically in what has been called its 'Cambrian explosion'.[5]

The Cambrian era, remember, was the geological period when it seems that life on earth exploded and spread rapidly across the planet. The self-esteem concept had its own 'Cambrian era', with a sudden increase in research and publications devoted to it. Twenge and Campbell have analysed data from scientific journals[6] to illustrate how, between 1967 and 1987, the annual number of publications on the topic of self-esteem quadrupled. By the turn of the millennium the self-esteem concept had spawned over 23,000 academic publications to become one of the top three topics in the whole of social psychology research.[7]

What gave the self-esteem idea such academic traction? As we saw in the last chapter, the first factor was self-esteem's ability to simplify the complex and highly nuanced ideas about self-regard that had been generated by the psychoanalysts. Whether you favoured Karen Horney's picture of the shrinking self, Freud's model of the punishing super-ego, or Adler's inferiority complex, they all seemed to point to something that had gone drastically wrong in the way that we think about ourselves; low self-worth was a relatively simple way of bringing it all together. So in the mid-1960s the psychologist Morris Rosenberg shaped the self-esteem concept around the idea of personal 'worthiness'.[8] He thought of it as a stable attitude towards yourself based on a perception of your overall value or 'worth'.

The second factor was the arrival of a flood of new rating scales. The most popular by far also happened to be developed by Morris Rosenberg.[9] The Rosenberg scale is a relatively cheap-and-cheerful ten-point self-completion tool that can be used with different types of people in different circumstances. If you need to check whether your own self-esteem is in good shape, it's readily available online.[10]

Psychologists *love* numbers, and now, with the Rosenberg scale, the self-esteem concept could be turned into one. Rating scales allowed the self-esteem idea to make a decisive move from the subjective and philosophical world of psychoanalysis to the precise, supposedly objective and scientific domain of empirical psychology. Just like any other objective 'thing' out there in the world around us, it could now be measured, scrutinized, manipulated and potentially altered. The 'thingification' (or reification) of self-esteem was complete, and, as psychologists increasingly used the term in academic discourse, we all began to think that now we knew exactly what we were talking about.

The next stepping-stone for its entry into the upper echelons of academic psychology was the idea that the 'wrong' amount of self-esteem – too little or too much – has profound psychological consequences. As Rosenberg's scale was used to test different kinds of people, researchers turned up a plethora of new and exciting links. It turned out that people with mental health problems as varied as anxiety, panic attacks, depression and anorexia nervosa had low self-esteem. Children with behaviour problems and low educational achievement reported low self-esteem. Teenagers who found themselves pregnant, had contracted sexually transmitted diseases or struggled with persistent relationship issues were found to have low self-esteem. Members of criminal gangs, alcoholics and drug addicts turned out to harbour low self-esteem. These discoveries suggested that we were homing in on a common causal factor for just about everything that psychologists, psychiatrists, educationalists and politicians worry about. And as Rosenberg's scale was rolled out in clinics, schools and youth clubs across America, the same findings just kept on coming.[11]

These were truly exciting findings, except for one fatal flaw: the belief that 'correlation equals causation'. 'Correlation' depends on the observation that two different events are linked together. Writing this book, for example, is strongly correlated with sitting at a desk here in my study. I rarely attempt to progress this book elsewhere, so whenever I am writing about self-esteem, you will find this beaten old desk lurking nearby. In fact, we are almost inseparable. So the correlation between sitting at this desk and writing this book is virtually 100%.

But would you conclude that the desk is 'causing' me to write the book? I doubt it. Yet this simple logical error – correlation equals causation – is committed by social science researchers over and over again. And in the case of self-esteem, this same logical flaw led to self-esteem being fingered as the culprit responsible for just about every kind of adversity that life throws at us.

The next, and perhaps the most powerful, catalyst of the academic Cambrian era was the huge potential for human flourishing offered by this field of research. With hindsight it is easy to see how psychologists and social scientists got so carried away. If low-esteem is bad for us, then boosting self-esteem must be good for us! Just think of the possibilities for prevention and for human flourishing if all of this had turned out to be true. Whole populations of children could be 'vaccinated' with programmes for boosting self-esteem. The new mode of thinking could be taught to children in their homes, schools and churches. 'Boosterism' was simple, straightforward to understand and readily marketable. And if it worked, modern psychology had truly stumbled upon the Holy Grail.

The Human Potential Movement

The final factor behind the academic success of self-esteem was the growth of new humanistic theories of human development among many of the big-name scholars and practitioners in modern psychology. Among them, Abraham Maslow, Rollo May and Carl Rogers were the high priests, the intellectual élite and the cultural innovators of what came to be known as the Human Potential Movement.

These new theorists loathed Freud's negative analysis of human motivation, especially his seeming obsession with sex and violence. Why had psychology been so seduced by the dark tide of Freudian pessimism, they asked? They distrusted the psychoanalysts' mechanistic approach to the mind that seemed to strip human beings of dignity. And they rejected the concept of a 'weak self', seemingly taken hostage by warring factions operating behind the scenes. The new humanists were determined to rehabilitate concepts of human dignity, worth and self-realization in modern psychology. And the self-esteem concept fitted it quite nicely.

Drawing inspiration from the work of philosophers suc[h]
Rousseau, and the artistic luminaries of the nineteenth-century
Romantic Movement such as Delacroix and Baudelaire,
Maslow and colleagues constructed grand optimistic scenarios
of human potential. They were less interested in what dragged
human thought down as in what built it up. And crucially, they
believed that, given the right conditions, the natural inclination
of the human psyche is towards growth, maturity and a life-
affirming desire for good.

Carl Rogers (who left a religious vocation at Union
Theological Seminary in New York to train as a psychologist
instead) was perhaps the most influential in terms of public
impact. His 'person-centred' approach birthed 'active
listening' and 'non-directive' counselling.[12] Rogers was
intrigued by the personal roots of Freud's pessimism. How
come Freud and he, both working intimately with clients in
distress, could experience people so differently, he asked?
Somebody was getting it wrong, and in his view it wasn't
Carl Rogers.

The culprit for Freud's pessimism, he decided, could be
found in the lonely and autistic nature of Freud's own self-
analysis. Put simply, Rogers believed that, with nobody to
provide him with the warmth and acceptance that he craved,
Freud had become locked into a dark cycle of pessimism and
negativity. So the idea was born in Rogers' mind that the route
to personal wholeness is achieved by being accepted, affirmed
and *listened to* by another person.

In Rogerian thought, it is the unconditional acceptance on
the part of the therapist that provides the healing nourish-
ment that frees us to accept ourselves unconditionally. Because
the human psyche is inherently disposed to a state of growth
and positive flourishing, the key task for the therapist is simply
to get the conditions right.

Of course, proponents of Rogers' ideas will argue that his position was far more nuanced and qualified than portrayed here. And regardless of what we think about Rogers' broader philosophy, clearly you can't begin to flourish psychologically when dark and unpalatable aspects of your own psyche are shuffled off, or worse, denied altogether. So let me state clearly that it is not possible to deal with an issue, or tackle a problem, unless and until you have accepted that it is *there*. In that sense, we all need to 'accept' ourselves. Understood like this, Rogers' argument for 'self-acceptance' is unexceptionable.

But that is not what Rogers was saying. Rogers held to the belief that the process of acceptance by the therapist has a 'releasing' quality. In a sense that I can only describe as mystical, he taught that the experience of being accepted by the therapist unleashes good in the human psyche: wholeness, growth, self-realization. He taught that the client ' . . . will find himself becoming better integrated, more able to function effectively; will become self-directing and self-confident; will become more of a person, more unique and more self-expressive; will be more understanding, more acceptant of others; will be able to cope with the problems of life more adequately and comfortably.'[13]

These are staggering assertions. Why should our human potential be inherently disposed towards good? Where is the evidence that the *process of acceptance itself* somehow unlocks the door to a change for the better? This isn't science; it's philosophy. As an article of faith, we may choose to believe that humans are in some way intrinsically patterned towards goodness, but there is little in the way of plausible evidence in scientific psychology to support such an assertion. And there is plenty of evidence in human history for believing otherwise. In his cogent analysis of the movement, the author and psychologist Paul Vitz called this 'psychology as religion'.[14]

His analysis still holds true for much of the person-centred counselling being pursued around the globe today.

And so the Cambrian era of self-esteem research, so much of which pivoted around the fallacy of 'correlation equals causation', helped to spawn powerful new schools of counselling, as well as countless research programmes and learned publications. But in the next stage of the story something remarkable happened that was to affect all our lives. Having achieved staggering success in the academy, the self-esteem idea now managed to break free from the confines of academia and professional counselling and get itself to the next level of popular culture. This happened because, in the late 1960s and the decade of the 1970s, self-esteem ideology achieved its *cultural* 'tipping point'.

Zeitgeist!

The self-esteem idea succeeded because it resonated perfectly with the emerging spirit of the age. In many ways, as a 1960s teenager I was a classic post-war baby boomer. We saw an unparalleled rise in prosperity, and, for the first time in history, much of that new money headed into our pockets. Our sheer weight of numbers created a vast new marketplace for the attention of advertisers and marketers. It made us feel 'special'. Indeed, as the author Steve Gillon observes, 'Almost from the time they were conceived, Boomers were dissected, analyzed, and pitched to by modern marketers who reinforced [their] sense of generational distinctiveness.'[15]

This sense of being distinctive or special was strengthened further in the new 'cool': cars and motorcycles; clothes and accessories; hairstyles and gadgets – all were designed with our needs in mind. And as the swagger of the grease-haired 1960s teenager with a radio pressed against his ear displaced the

1950s nuclear family cosily gathered for *Listen with Mother*, the transistor radio became a powerful icon of a new era.

The age of the individualist had arrived. From now on it was 'do your own thing', 'go with the flow' and 'let it all hang out'. No longer interested in the strictures of the past, what mattered to us was speaking from the heart, getting in touch with your true feelings and being yourself. In 1967, during the infamous 'Summer of Love', thousands of hippies descended on San Francisco with (literally) flowers in their hair. A few months before at a Golden Gate 'Human Be-In', Timothy Leary had urged people to 'turn on, tune in and drop out'. And as we groped in the dark, we stumbled across something familiar . . . Me!

Romanticism redux

Although we didn't realize it at the time, there was nothing particularly new in all of this. Humans had been here before, most recently in the Romantic Movement of the nineteenth century. Like us, the nineteenth-century Romantics had also reacted to a kind of austerity, in their case the formality and rationalism of the Enlightenment. And so the movement's artists, writers and composers embarked on an orgy of un-fettered emotion and self-expression.

The Romantics believed in the surrender of the rational to the 'deep-interior' of the human psyche. Artists such as Delacroix wanted to free themselves from the bonds of reason: 'When we surrender ourselves entirely to the soul it unfolds itself completely to us, and it is then that this capricious spirit grants us the greatest happiness of all . . . the joy of expressing the soul in a hundred different ways, of revealing it to others . . . '[16] Fast forward a century to the street language of the late 1960s and '70s, and Delacroix might have enjoined us to 'let it all hang out' and just 'go with the flow'.

But here is the riddle. Although the nineteenth-century Romantics had a huge impact on what we might call 'high culture', their vision never broke through into popular culture. It emerged briefly a few decades later, most notably in the 1920s, but it was never able to *make it* into popular culture in any sustained kind of way. So why, this time around, did these same ideas achieve such a lasting impact? Why was the 'new Romanticism' of the 1960s and '70s so successful? And how did it manage to shape the mindset of a generation and transform a culture?

I would not embark on a prolonged cultural analysis, even if I were capable of it. My central point, however, is that the new Romanticism succeeded where the previous Romanticism had failed because it was effectively 'baptized' with science – the new psychology of self-esteem. In other words, although the tipping point of self-esteem had been triggered by the cultural conditions of the 1960s, the movement that resulted now ensured that those same conditions were perpetuated, through the 1980s, the 1990s and into the new millennium. This was a cultural paradigm shift, and the legacy is every-where around us today. And it's due to an unholy amalgam of psychological science and the growing cultural narcissism.

We see this most clearly in some of the films of the 1970s, as a new generation of 'philosopher scriptwriters' began to weave together the language of the 'deep interior' with the language of therapy. *Kramer vs. Kramer*, released in 1979, is one of the most potent examples of this genre.

As the opening credits fade, we witness the pale, pained profile of Joanna Kramer, a young mother, played by Meryl Streep. Slowly, as the camera moves away from her vacant gaze, we see that she is rubbing the back of a small boy called

Billie. It's bedtime. 'Don't let the bugs bite,' his mother whispers. 'I'll see you in the morning light,' responds Billie.

But in the morning light Billie's mother will be gone. After leaving the bedroom, she slowly, methodically packs her suitcase. When her husband Ted (played by Dustin Hoffman) arrives home later that evening, Joanna tells him that she doesn't love him any more. Her bags are packed and she is ready to go. He and Billie will be better off without her. As Joanna walks out of the house and disappears from the frame, the viewer is left shocked, indeed stunned, that a mother could ever contemplate such a thing.

Much of what follows is taken up with Ted's learning curve as the reluctant carer of this newly abandoned and deeply vulnerable young boy. But later in the film Joanna re-emerges. Now she is confident and composed. And she wants her son back.

We learn how she had needed to find and accept herself, and that now, after therapy, she is ready once again to be a mother. Some commentators accuse the film-makers of exhuming the well-worn Hollywood theme of a woman escaping domestic drudgery to find work and love. I disagree. These philosopher scriptwriters were more subtle and challenging than that. They were telling us that, amidst the ambiguities of a mother walking out on a vulnerable young boy, there is something fundamentally right, perhaps even morally imperative, about her actions. *Kramer vs. Kramer* cemented the thought that would eventually define a generation: you cannot love others until first you have learned to love yourself. Now, thirty years later, how many people would disagree with that?

Through the 1980s a string of movies explored the theme of self-discovery further. We were urged to 'feel the force' (don't think about it) and 'trust your feelings'. Dr Spock's austere and logical flattening of the emotions was so out of kilter with culture that it simply re-enforced the point: If you are looking for a happy and fulfilled life, 'go with the flow' and 'be yourself'. In the movie, *Dead Poets Society*, the tragic suicide of a teenager who had been emotionally shackled by his parents warned about the dire consequences of doing anything else.

But it took George Lucas's *Star Wars* movie to capture the final ascendency of the Self. Arriving at the finale, our two heroes are seen walking proudly through a vast, cheering crowd of admirers. Now, having learned to trust their feelings, they are about to be awarded with the highest prize of all: the acclaim of the people, the approval of their peers and the worship of the masses. The Self has triumphed. It is no longer simply a part of some greater story; the Self *is* the story. And here, receiving the acclaim of its peers, it may be found at the very pinnacle of where it wants to be.

Nothing could stop it now. The stage was set. Underpinned with the 'science' of self-esteem, the new Romantic Movement would outlast all that had gone before. We arrived in the 1980s, when Gordon Gecko declared, 'Greed is good' and Mrs Thatcher famously announced that 'there is no such thing as society'. We turn now to explore how, over the next two decades, with the wind in its sails, the self-esteem idea continued its work in popular culture, in our schools and colleges, in our law courts and our mental health services. And, most cleverly of all, how it got to work on our Christian faith.

3. CATCH THEM YOUNG AND SELL IT HARD

See Yourself As Goddess. Begin to notice your perfections when you look in the mirror. Receive compliments as graciously and copiously as you give them. Say 'yes, yes, YES' a lot, with revellious and delightful energy. Practice shameless acts of joy and master joyous acts of shame. Affirm yourself daily with delicious words including 'magical, mystical, sparkling, juicy, ethereal, beauty, intuitive, divine.' When you see yourself as Goddess, this is the gorgeous energy you radiate and hence, you begin to attract similarly gorgeous people into your life.
'How to Marry Yourself'[1]

So self-esteem ideology not only entwined itself with the culture changes of the 1960s and '70s, it rolled up its sleeves to drive and sustain them. It did this through a virtual hijacking of the self-help industry and a highly successful penetration of the educational establishment. Let's see how this worked.

The democratization of self-esteem

In the US much of the early self-help spadework was carried forward by the National Council for Self-Esteem, and then by the National Association for Self-Esteem (NASE).[2] NASE's mission is 'to fully integrate self-esteem into the fabric of American society so that every individual, no matter what their age or background, experiences personal worth and happiness'.[3]

Despite a burgeoning army of experts and counsellors, the scale of self-esteem ideology's ambition meant that it would have to teach us to help ourselves. I am not commenting on the quality or effectiveness of any particular programme, but on the NASE website, for example, you can download a whole month's supply of 'daily inspiration' cards for sticking on your lunch pack. As you peel your banana and sip your cappuccino, you can munch happily to the thought: 'Dream big!'; 'You are something special'; 'I'm proud of you!' And yes, 'You're incredible!'[4]

We are urged to repeat these kinds of statements several times a day, especially at night before going to bed and when rising in the morning. But don't be in a hurry! We are advised to take it slowly and experience positive feelings with each statement. There's a sort of self-esteem 'quiet time' too, with advice to set aside an hour each morning for 'personal development matters'. And in what is described as a 'powerful strategy for self-renewal', we are urged to take time to reflect, visualize our day, read inspirational texts and listen to motivational tapes.[5]

As self-esteem worked to get these kinds of messages out, the self-help industry was soon churning out vast quantities of manuals, workbooks, websites, DVDs, mentoring programmes and life-changing seminars. In the world of self-help, every angle was covered and no stone left unturned. In a hurry? Then get hold of *Ten Days to Self-Esteem*. Short of options? Then discover *200 Ways to Raise a Girl's Self-Esteem*. It's a boy? No worries, there are *100 Ways to Raise a Boy's Self-Esteem*. Not your problem? Then discover the joys of

Building Your Mates' Self-Esteem! With so much on offer, you can *Restore Your Magnificence, Honour Yourself* and curl up with *A Girl's Guide to Loving Herself Inside Out.* The possibilities are endless. With the self-help industry, the democratization of self-esteem was well and truly under way.

Catch them young

Self-esteem ideology was also wildly successful in capturing the educational establishments of both the United States and much of Europe. It began in 1986 when Governor George Deukmejian of California signed into law a piece of legislation creating 'The State Task Force to Promote Self-Esteem and Personal and Social Responsibility'. This State-sponsored study group, which comprised hundreds of scholars and policy makers, was charged with discovering how self-esteem could be spread at mass-population scale to penetrate every level of society.[6]

The creation of the California Task Force inaugurated the concept of 'therapeutic education', and probably had more impact in catalysing the booster movement and multiplying the number of self-esteem experts than any other factor in American culture at that time. As a result, the 'need' for good self-esteem soon peppered the conversations of teachers and school governors, curriculum planners and school counsellors. It became the focus of questions at parents' evenings. If self-esteem is so good for you, how do we make sure that our children are getting enough? Is the school taking the right approach? How can we nurture and promote it at home and in church? And if good self-esteem is the key to avoiding problems like bulimia and depression when we get older, how can we prevent these problems before they occur? Will there be enough psychologists and counsellors to go round? And can we afford it? You can feel the panic setting in.

The key was prevention, delivered as early and as effectively as possible. So the California Task Force invented the concept of a 'social vaccine', in which boosterism would be delivered through systematic educational intervention. Soon schools became the happy hunting grounds for a new breed of 'conceptual entrepreneurs', an army of consultants and counsellors dedicated to the task of helping teachers in their new responsibilities towards the young hearts and minds that had been placed in their charge.

While I make no comment about the quality or relative effectiveness of any particular programme, the Power of Positive Students (POPS) International Foundation,[7] under the leadership of Dr William Mitchell, an educationalist, is one example of how self-esteem was rolled out into the education system. It is claimed that these resources have been used by over one million students in 5,000 US schools, in all fifty States, and in twelve different countries worldwide.[8] POPS believes that students 'must learn to believe in themselves, to like who they are and to feel that they make a difference . . . ' The blurb goes on: 'But how do we make sure that everybody knows just how important he is? A comprehensive school/community programme focusing on staff development and community involvement has been designed by POPS to meet this challenge.'[9]

In Australia it was the (potentially important) perception that girls suffer from disproportionately low self-esteem that helped to promote boosterism in schools.[10] Over the next few years there was a positive flourishing of new educational reform schemes, consultancies and curriculum design centres focused on this task.[11]

Self-esteem ideology became the key to big money as well:

> Given its popularity, self-esteem can be a powerful term for people to use in their quest for public acceptance (and financial support) . . . and it is now possible to identify a variety of programmes which use self-esteem as an organising concept, even when self-esteem is not, strictly speaking, what the project is about.[12]

In other words, researchers and educational 'consultants' started to talk up the need for self-esteem to seduce fund-holders into releasing the money. Such studies involved putting small groups of girls together for a range of exotic activities, including building collages of self, mapping auto-biographical timelines, creating personal silhouettes and carrying out various fantasy and self-visualization exercises. The girls also got involved in interactive exercises, such as rehearsing compliments, standing up for their rights, and assertiveness training. And with resources such as *Self-Esteem: A Classroom Affair – 101 Ways to Help Children Like Themselves*,[13] the educational arm of the self-help industry soon came running to meet everybody's needs.

Similar programmes have been mainstreamed in a UK government educational initiative called the SEAL (Social and Emotional Aspects of Learning) Project. First published in 2005, SEAL was soon being rolled out across the state educational system. In a structured programme designed to be delivered year on year to children between the ages of three and eighteen, SEAL aimed to put the teaching of social and emotional skills at the very heart of education. Although voluntary, it is designed to be delivered with a full pack of teaching resources, and pupils' progress can be mapped against highly specified targets and outcomes. And of course, building good self-esteem is right up there among them.[14]

We need to be careful to distinguish baby from bathwater here. There is much that is good in the desire to equip our children and young people to handle their emotions and build personal resilience. We should applaud efforts to combat bullying and instil confidence on the back of hard work and genuine talent. The danger, however, is that, given the strength and potency of self-esteem ideology, these other messages all too easily get lost or ignored. And even helpful efforts to combat self-hatred and low self-worth can, unless they are part of something that lifts our sights beyond ourselves, all too easily spill over into the cult of celebrity and self-admiration.

The many sides of self-admiration

All of this activity in self-help and education meant that the original alliance forged between self-esteem ideology and the new Romanticism of the 1960s and 1970s was spectacularly successful. Indeed, although self-esteem had a natural ally in its early cultural partners, it displayed a remarkable capacity to adapt, chameleon-like, to equally profound cultural shifts in the decades that followed. It made a relatively smooth and seamless transition, for example, from the long-haired drop-out culture of the bearded 1970s to the materialistic orgies of the 1980s. And then, with the 1990s and the dawn of a new millennium, we hardly noticed its deft interweaving with more subtle and nuanced forms of greed: a growing preoccupation with rights and entitlement, a fixation with celebrity and image, the shallow emotionality of self-pity and 'recreational grief'.[15]

Self-esteem ideology soon spread beyond the USA too. Great Britain, which had contributed so much to the cultural changes that catalysed the movement in the 1960s, proved a ready receptacle, as self-esteem thinking fanned out from the States and across Western culture. The fall of the Iron Curtain in the early 1990s allowed it to begin its work of cultural change in former Eastern bloc countries too.

By the new millennium the culture of self was so embedded that we barely noticed it any more. In 2004 Alexandra Robbins' book, *Conquering Your Quarterlife Crisis*, told us about a young man called Jason. Jason had decided that big changes were required in his philosophy of life. So what was his new motto? What could rescue him from the encircling gloom of life as a twenty-something? 'Do your best for Jason. I had to make me happy; I had to do what was best for me, in every situation.'[16] How many people would disagree with that now? Switch on your television and you hear it all the time. Me!

In 2004 Britney Spears announced that she was quitting the music business. Just back from her honeymoon, she had new fish to fry and different priorities to pursue: 'Myself, my husband, Kevin, and starting a family'.[17] Note the order. Me!

By the new millennium the culture of self was so embedded that we barely noticed it any more.

On Friday 23 June 2006, frantic last-minute preparations were under way for a bizarre ceremony due to take place the next day.[18] After recovering from an exhausting 'stagette', seven brides-to-be were reported to be looking forward to the big event the following afternoon. Arriving with white veils flowing in the wind aboard a convertible red Cadillac, the seven breathless brides were going to take their vows barefoot on the beach. Afterwards they planned to swoon back to a lavish gourmet picnic with white linens.

Great fun, and why not? But when the women threw back their veils to take their vows, they affirmed a lifelong commitment to love, honour and cherish – themselves. With this ring I me wed! The idea had finally been born that, to be happy, secure and prosperous, to be a woman, to be a whole person, first you need to marry yourself. Me!

Because of the success of the self-esteem industry, the phenomenon of 'me first' resonates all around us, from cyclists who ignore traffic lights, through to those who throw litter on the streets, to parents who scheme, manipulate and bully to get their children into the best schools but refuse to serve as school governors themselves.

But does a collection of anecdotes like this really prove anything? Haven't we always tended to think that 'young people today' are going to the dogs? How much of a cultural shift has there really been, and where exactly is the objective evidence?

Ego tracking

In 2006 the respected UK Henley Centre for Forecasting disclosed findings from a tracking poll that had been posing the same set of questions for over twenty years. Each year the pollsters had asked, 'Do you think the quality of life in Britain is best improved by (a) looking after the community's interests instead of our own or (b) looking after ourselves, which ultimately raises standards for all?'

Before the year 2000 the overwhelming majority had chosen (a). Most people thought that the best way to improve the quality of life for everybody was to put other people's interests ahead of their own. But as a new millennium dawned, the gap began to close. And just six years later a majority (53%) of those interviewed chose option (b). For the first time in the history of the poll more people believed in looking after 'me' first.[19]

Another Henley Centre survey speaks of the 'ruthless pursuit of self-interest in a climate of competitiveness', and a 'new environment of entitlement' in which everyone has the right to a good job and all the perks that go with it.[20]

Of course, it's important not to oversimplify these types of data. People may now simply be more honest about reporting their views, compared with previous decades. And there are still extraordinary examples of selflessness and community involvement among young and old too.[21] But that's not the point. The point is that such examples are becoming the exception rather than the rule.

We observe the same patterns in the USA. The American psychologist Jean M. Twenge has done some ground-breaking work by constructing tracking polls covering periods of nearly half a century. Her book *Generation Me* is a scholarly and gripping introduction to her work. Twenge developed a fairly simple, but incredibly time-consuming, method. First, she rooted out all the surveys that had used roughly the same measurement instrument over the past forty or fifty years. Then she set about analysing them, sifting out the best quality studies and making various statistical adjustments. Finally, she compared her findings across several decades and illustrated them visually in time-graphs. In fact, she estimates that she 'probably pulled half a million journals off the shelves'.[22]

What did Twenge discover? In one study[23] she found that, by the mid-1990s, the *average* male college student had a higher self-esteem than had 86% of male college students back in 1968. At the end of the study period, college students were much more likely to agree with statements such as 'I take a positive attitude towards myself' and 'on the whole, I am satisfied with myself'.

Twenge linked her findings with other surveys that mirrored this trend. In one survey carried out in the 1990s 91% of teens described themselves as 'responsible', 74% believed they were 'physically attractive' and 79% reported themselves to be 'very intelligent'.[24] Another found that, in the early 1950s, only 12% of teens aged fourteen to sixteen agreed with the statement: 'I am an important person.' By the late 1980s, however, a staggering 80% claimed to feel important in this way. Compared with previous generations, post-millennial college students were also much more likely to agree with statements such as, 'I find it easy to manipulate people' and 'I insist upon getting the respect that is due to me.'[25]

What about children? By the 1980s children's self-esteem was also taking a sharp turn upwards. Increasingly, kids were agreeing with statements such as, 'I'm easy to like' and 'I always do the right thing.' Despite escalating divorce rates and family breakdown, the average child in the mid-1990s had higher self-esteem than 73% of kids in 1979. So, despite continuing social instability, why did children's self-esteem increase so dramatically during the 1980s and 1990s? Twenge's answer is simple: therapeutic education and the rise of the self-esteem curriculum. And her conclusion overall? 'Today's young Americans are more confident, assertive, entitled – and more miserable than ever before.'[26]

More *miserable* than ever before? Hang on a moment. Is that right? Have I reported Twenge accurately here? Today's young Americans are more . . . 'mentally healthy', 'psychologically stable' and 'socially integrated', surely? Wasn't that the whole point of the self-esteem project? Didn't it promise to make us healthy, wealthy and wise? Twenge seems to believe that not only are Americans no better off after the self-esteem project, but, in mental health terms at least, they are actually *worse off.*

We have arrived at the point where we need to ask the $64,000 question: *Does it work?* After four decades of the self-esteem movement, how does the evidence stack up? And is there really evidence, as Twenge asserts, that it has even done more harm than good? But first there's one last facet of self-admiration to be explored. How did self-esteem ideology impact upon the life of the church?

4. TO GOD YOU'RE BIG STUFF!

The woman smiled at me.
'Jesus is the perfect playmate,'
she said.
Tanya Luhrmann, Field notes, Spring 2008[1]

A recent Gallup Poll in the weekly magazine Newsweek
reports that nearly 80% of Americans believe there is a
heaven and that they are destined to go there,
whereas only 7% believe that there is a hell and
that they are likely to end up there . . .
Heaven is simply one more entitlement that no one,
presumably even God, has a right to deny us.
Donald Capps, Princeton Theological Seminary[2]

In the 1970s a new children's song burst onto the Christian scene. 'The Butterfly Song' had children everywhere thanking their heavenly Father for making me – Me! The logic went something like this: if we were butterflies, we'd be grateful to God for making us so colourful; and if we were fish, we would jump in the water with happiness, so . . . because God gives us things like eyes and feet and smiles, we should simply thank him for making me . . . Me![3]

So what's the problem with that? The words of this song are no more remarkable than any other celebrating God's goodness in creation and his delight in his children. But 'The Butterfly Song' actually marked a startling departure from our previous diet of children's choruses. And it made Christians sit up and take notice. Until now our Sunday school songs and chorus lines conveyed sentiments such as:

For He is our childhood's pattern;
Day by day, like us He grew;
He was little, weak and helpless,
Tears and smiles, like us He knew . . .[4]

How should little Christian children be? Why, 'mild, obedient, good as He' of course. We sang ditties such as 'Jesus first, yourself last, and others in between', and songs with words like, 'Little ones to Him belong; they are weak but He is strong.'

These lyrics sound gratingly out of kilter with modern culture. Me last? Surely not! Weak, helpless, mild and obedient? What kind of recipe is that for building a kid's self-confidence? Back in the 1970s 'The Butterfly Song' provided an assertive, confident, self-affirming lyric that chimed perfectly with the emerging culture of the Me generation. For Christians too the time had now arrived to cast off the legacy of guilt-laden children's anthems inherited from our Victorian forebears and begin to love ourselves just like the rest of the world.

What was going on here? These changes in Christian tradition are traceable to the cultural revolution of the 1960s and the Me decade of the 1970s, similar to today's secular self-admiration. In other words, as these social trends unfolded in broader society, they impacted progressively on Christian culture too. All too often Christians appear to be limping along behind secular change, rather than setting the pace in distinctive counter-cultural thought, and our mindless piggy-backing onto the self-esteem movement remains one of the most potent examples of our intellectual vulnerability to the latest 'thing'.

User-friendly Jesus

In the wake of the San Francisco Summer of Love, young Christians began to discover the radical outsider in Jesus of Nazareth too. Why, with his long hair and free-flowing garments, Jesus even looked like a hippy! In a compelling analysis of the explosive growth of American (and Western) experiential evangelicalism over the past four decades, the anthropologist Tanya Luhrmann suggests that the process began as worried evangelists reached out to hippies who had got themselves into trouble.[5] Hungry to build bridges and generate links with their lifestyle, they appealed to these young revolutionaries by suggesting that they could refocus their rebellion around the iconic, long-haired, sandal-footed carpenter from Galilee.

Meanwhile in secular culture, after the ground-breaking rock musical *Hair*, Jesus musicals like *Godspell* and *Jesus Christ Superstar* (both back on Broadway in 2012) were coming onto the scene. In *Godspell* we join a hippy romp through Matthew's Gospel, with Jesus sporting a Superman shirt under bright trouser braces, frizzy hair and the psychedelic orange slippers of a clown. As his chilled-out hippy tribe of disciples bounce around the stage with him, he smears paint on their faces and tells them that God loves them.

Here, says Luhrmann, is a user-friendly Jesus: 'For sure, he strode into the temple and overthrew the money changers – but you were there at his side, a counter-cultural revolutionary.

He did not thunder at *you*. You and he stood together, challenging *them*. And when you were not in the temple together, he was a peaceful, happy, zany Godspell God, infinitely patient, infinitely accepting, a God of endless love.'[6]

This was the Jesus who was soon being offered by the new spiritual communes and coffee houses springing up all over the country. The Jesus Freaks flocked inside and tweaked their nickname to become – the Jesus People. And as the movement mushroomed (in more ways than one), drug-fuelled 'be-ins' gave way to 'turn-off, tune-in, drop-out' nights with Jesus. In 'psychedelic-haloed images of Jesus in grainy photojournalism shots of mass baptisms in the oceans',[7] the Jesus People even found their way onto the covers of *Life* and *Time*.

Here was a God who would 'hold your hand, wipe your brow, and get you through a bad trip . . . '[8] Luhrmann tells how, in 2008 during the course of her fieldwork, she met Sally, 'an old Jesus person, someone who had danced with Jesus and who let the electric excitement of the Holy Spirit take the place of drugs'. Sally came from a conventional middle-class Washington suburb, but soon found herself being drawn into drug culture and the Sergeant Pepper lifestyle that went with it.

But Sally was now troubled by the dark underbelly of the movement:

> We were marching against the war, we were involved in the civil rights movement, we were burning bras, we were having lie-ins where we'd all sort of sit around and make out. Yeah, it was political. But when it got to this other level [she witnessed a friend who broke down on LSD and had to be hospitalized, and another so wasted he peed on the couch], it was not political. It was kinky, bad, self-destructive, and scary, and I didn't like it.

One evening a neighbour invited her to church, where, in contrast to her previous 'dry-sex' experience of institutional religion, she encountered a minister who was 'just on fire'. 'He looked me sort of right in the eye, and he said, "Would you like to be whole?" And I said, "Whole, oh, that sounds really, really, good."' Luhrmann concludes, 'That was it. For the next ten years, she was one of the hippie Christians, and her life revolved around the Bible. It really was, she said, like living in *Godspell*: "All love and little or no judgment. No rules. Very little structure. Tons of humour. It was *sooo* seductive."'[9]

In many ways, just as the bizarre encounter sessions and psychological 'be-ins' of the 1970s, described by authors such as Tom Wolfe, were caricatures to alert us to the more general cultural shifts of the 'Me decade', the antics of the Jesus Movement and the *Godspell* followers may also be viewed as the tip of an iceberg: indicators of more profound and subtle shifts taking place in wider Christian culture too.

Perfect in his eyes

Slowly, gradually, the Self was being moved to the centre of the story in Christian culture, in the same way that it had repositioned itself in secular culture. We no longer wanted to sing, 'Tell me the old, old story' but rather, 'Let me tell you my story!' Self-esteem ideology colonized the Christian world with the same absorption with self, my needs, my Saviour, my salvation, Me! as everywhere else. We baptized the 'greed is good' of Gordon Gekko with our own version called the 'prosperity gospel'. The sentimentalities and entitlements of the 1990s were mirrored in our own version of solution-styled gospel. The Christ of the Bible was progressively edited, *Godspell* style, to become 'Jesus, the perfect playmate'.[10]

And as the self-esteem movement democratized itself through the self-help industry, Christians developed their own self-help industry too, especially in the USA. There were soon scores of Christian self-esteem resources, with titles like *Perfect in His Eyes*[11] and 10 *Steps to Revolutionize Your Life: Finally a Book for Building Self-Esteem that is Biblically Based, Full of Practical Things to Do, and Truly Life Changing*.[12] Forget 'we are weak but he is strong'; now you could get the T-shirt: 'I may be little, but to God I'm big stuff!'

Although it wasn't published until 1997, the title of the influential and top-selling children's book, *You Are Special* by Max Lucado,[13] is a good example of this new perspective. In fact, you can now treat yourself to an upgrade with *Best of All!*[14] Let me be clear, there are some very, very good ideas in this book, which uses an imaginative storyline to encourage children to turn down the different 'labels' that others try to stick on them. This point is important and biblical, and I am not advocating throwing out the baby with the bathwater.

But what interests me here is the subtle shift in tone seen in the choice of titles, the focus on 'me' and the generous helpings of words such as 'special' and 'best'. How much of this is a legitimate reappraisal of the balance of Scripture in relation to how children can be encouraged to flourish psychologically? And how much is a simple aping of popular culture and the cult of self, with the same potential side-effects of self-admiration?

Astonishingly, some Christians, limping along behind popular culture, have managed to take self-esteem ideology one step further in theological terms too. Before you can even love God, they claim, you need to love yourself: 'Self-love is thus the prerequisite and the criterion for our conduct towards our neighbour . . . You cannot love neighbour, you cannot love God, unless you first love yourself.'[15]

And finally, the cross itself is turned into just another symbol of self-worth. Doesn't God love us with such a passion that it took his Son to the cross? Then we must be *worth saving*. So even the cross of Christ is made the servant of our quest for self-esteem.

Pick-and-mix religion

The logic of self-approval has led to a suspicion of other aspects of traditional Christian spirituality too. We disapprove of the old 'shoulds' and 'should nots' that imposed such limits on choice and individuality. As part of this, we now take a more relaxed view of Sunday worship, downgrading the church twice-on-Sunday mentality to a more friendly pick-and-mix approach that suits our chosen lifestyle. Teenagers are especially vulnerable to a take-your-pick approach to faith, cruising through their teens sampling a little here and a little there, much as they will cruise fresher fairs when they arrive at university looking for the biggest and the best.[16]

Wade Clark Roof, who has been studying the religious journey of baby boomers since the mid-1980s, describes these changing perspectives on religion as a 'radical shift from an ethic of self-denial to an ethic of self-fulfilment'. This results in a religion 'functionally and spatially located in the self . . . Individuals are free to create their own religious faith and consecrate their own sacred space . . . This kind of religious individualist neither wants, nor feels the need for, formal religious institutions.'[17] Thus, in one wide-ranging study carried out by University of California sociologists, the authors tell of a woman named Sheila who invented and then practised her very own religion. Its creed and liturgical structures were so unique that she named the religion after herself: 'Sheilaism', explaining, 'It's just try to love yourself and be gentle with yourself.'[18]

Church for narcissists

As a consequence of our obsession with choice and individuality, many of the most successful and growing churches have made far-reaching adaptations in their 'offer'. I was once part of a congregation where the minister berated us for failing to be in our seats precisely by the time the service started, and singing hymns and songs while slouched with our hands in our pockets. This did not go down at all well! At the time it was, at worst, an ill-judged remark; now such an intervention would be totally laughable.

Most growing churches today positively *play* to our culture's preference for informality and individuality. While mainline denominations with their regimented services and predictable liturgies wither on the vine, these churches greet you with freshly brewed coffee, a slice of lemon drizzle cake and a choice of seating that ranges from white leather settees, through hard-backed chairs to cushions scattered around the floor. No worries if you prefer to sit through the first few songs and leave crumbs on the floor. In fact it's positively encouraged. And who cares if you need the toilet during the prayers?

After a PowerPoint-based inspirational talk interspersed with uplifting stories of a failing marriage that has been turned around, sore backs that have been healed and holiday money found in an envelope that just 'popped' through the door, you can 'respond' in any way you like: stay in your seat in quiet meditation, wander up to the front for prayer ministry, stand and sing with your arms raised.

Authors Jennifer Twenge and Keith Campbell, in their highly original investigation of what they consider to be our current epidemic of narcissism, argue that today's most successful churches have adapted cleverly to our self-orientated culture by front-ending their appeal with what people want. Their services offer optimal choice and effectively demand nothing. They cite Lakewood Church in Houston, Texas, the largest church in the United States, led by the successful author and pastor, Joel Osteen:

> Lakewood is clearly giving the people what they want.
> 'God didn't create you to be average,' Osteen writes (leaving unanswered the pertinent question: If God doesn't want anyone to be average, doesn't that change the average?). 'You were made to excel. You were made to leave your mark on this generation . . . Start [believing] I've been chosen, set apart, destined to live in victory,' writes Osteen in his book *Become a Better You*.[19]

Twenge and Campbell suggest that Osteen 'clearly practices the self-admiration he preaches; the walls of Lakewood Church are covered with perfectly airbrushed pictures of Osteen and plaques quoting his words.' 'Some of his advice verges on narcissistic acquisitiveness, such as when he suggests that we should all be expressing our wants, as his son was when he received the new guitar he wanted and immediately asked, "When do you think we can get my new keyboard?"!'[20]

But Twenge and Campbell offer an important insight by suggesting that there is a flip side to Osteen's message that is 'almost a course in anti-narcissism'. 'The second half of *Become a Better You* [says], "Praise people as much as you can, swallow your pride and apologise, let strife out of your life, build better relationships."'[21] Their central point is that successful churches 'connect' with people's narcissism, but then attempt to draw them into something larger than themselves, back into a religious worldview: 'This odd bit of alchemy – taking narcissism and trying to turn it into altruism – is at the heart of much modern religion.'[22]

I think there is something in this argument, but it is a high-risk strategy. In a scholarly and far-reaching analysis of the highly successful Willow Creek 'seeker' model in the US, Greg Pritchard warns that, while adopting the psychological language of popular culture may well enable our churches to identify with the unchurched, church discourse conducted in 'psychological categories' results in churches full of people with 'psychological identities'. As a consequence, 'the goals and means of one's ethics change from a God-centred to a human-centred orientation'.[23] In other words, when you talk like a pop psychologist, you begin to think like one.

There are great risks here for leaders too, especially those who lack the wisdom and peer support to detect the intoxicating effects of celebrity. Once churchgoers have become accustomed to a weekly Sunday service that plays to their natural inclination towards self-admiration, altruistic messages are unlikely to impact in any significant way upon habits of the heart that have been constructed and rehearsed for the previous six days and twenty-three hours. We need a more open, honest and challenging debate about narcissism and the cult of self in modern church life, and pastors do us few favours by simply aping our hearts' desires.

Later we will return to some of the theological questions that the self-esteem movement poses. But now we need to return to the issue we left dangling at the conclusion of the last chapter. Two major questions remain unanswered. While the self-esteem movement has been spectacularly successful, in Christian and secular cultures alike, at getting the self to centre stage, we still don't know whether it *worked*. Has it actually produced the human and social goods it promised? Are we happier, more psychologically stable, more relational and better socially integrated? If not, then more worryingly, could self-esteem ideology have done more harm than good?

5. DOES BOOSTERISM WORK?

When teens turn to risky sexual behaviour to cope with their feelings, it creates many of what we consider our society's ills: teen pregnancy, abortion, sexually transmitted disease, and the breakdown of traditional marriage and family. Teens are not usually mature enough to cope with the very real risks and responsibilities of sexual behaviour. Why do people do it? Broken down to a very simple level, these conditions all stem from depression and low self-esteem. These teens feel badly about themselves and desperately need love and approval.
Teen Self-Esteem and Sex Facts:
A Factsheet for Parents of Troubled Teens[1]

Does this factsheet – a tribute to the success of the self-esteem movement in getting out its message – contain reliable facts?

These are bold claims, laying the blame for a staggering array of teenage problems – unwanted pregnancies, abortion, sexually transmitted diseases, even the breakdown of traditional marriage and family – firmly at the door of 'depression and low self-esteem'. But as we saw in chapter 3, tracking data show remarkable improvements in self-esteem over the past three decades. Compared with those young people who witnessed the election of Britain's first woman prime minister in 1979, young people today are more, much more, gorgeous in their own eyes. Everywhere you look, people are trying to feel good about themselves, whether in school, college, the workplace or church. The health benefits should be stacking up all around us. So has this radical change in self-perception delivered the promised goods?

To unearth the answer to this, we need the help of an American psychologist called Roy Baumeister and a British academic called Nicholas Emler, from the London School of Economics. Baumeister was once a big fan of self-esteem, but in 2003 the American Psychological Society invited him to carry out a far-reaching and comprehensive review of all the hard evidence that had been gathered to date. His work remains one of the most cogent and robust critiques of the self-esteem movement available.[2] And Nicholas Emler carried out a similar review for the Joseph Rowntree Foundation in the UK.[3] What did they find?

Gorgeous in our own eyes

First, Roy Baumeister pointed out how tricky it is to measure the kind of attitudes and behaviours that are said to benefit from boosting self-esteem.[4] The most widely used tools simply rely on what the subject tells you. This is pretty worrying, as there is plenty of evidence that relying on what people say about themselves can often be way off the mark. When we talk about ourselves, especially to an attractive young researcher, we like to look good at the time and feel better afterwards.

One study, for example, showed that people with *high* self-esteem tend to rate themselves as more physically attractive.[5] When objective judges were asked to score their attractiveness, however, the link between the subject's own reported level of esteem and their attractiveness to the judges fell virtually to zero. In other words, those with high self-esteem are 'gorgeous in their own eyes but not necessarily so to others'.[6]

People with high self-regard tend to think that they are more popular and sociable too. But when researchers asked 542 ninth-grade students to nominate their most-liked peers, the correlation with the students' own ratings of their popularity was once again close to zero.[7] College students with high self-regard also consider themselves to be brilliant at making new friends, better at supporting old friends, more open and assertive, and more skilled in conflict management. Ask their room-mates what they think, however, and you get a different picture.

And what about their love lives? On the face of it, we would expect people with poor self-regard to be more worried about rejection and to have less durable relationships. But researchers found that, while youngsters with low self-esteem find it hard to trust other people and tend to fear rejection, there is no evidence that their relationships are actually more prone to break up. In fact, one study showed that people with high self-regard are more likely to respond to a hitch in their relationships by disposing of their partner and using their well-oiled social skills to get themselves a new one instead![8]

Finding the culprit

In the next stage of his investigation, Roy Baumeister turned to the question of unravelling cause and effect. In other words, how can we figure out whether low self-esteem really does cause all of those problems set out in the fact sheet quoted above, or whether it's all just correlation? When things go wrong, how can we tell whether low self-esteem really is the culprit?

Even where objective (as opposed to self-reported) measures are used, the fallacy that disfigures much of the research in this area, as we saw earlier, is the assumption that *correlation* is the same thing as *causation*. Sitting at the desk in front of me right now is strongly correlated with writing this book, remember, but is it actually causing me to do it? I think not.

Even an apparent link between two factors may not be as straightforward as it appears. A study might show that members of the British Conservative Party are more satisfied with their sex lives than members of the Labour Party. So should we all join the Conservatives then? A couple of points require our attention first. If men generally tend to report being more satisfied with their sex lives than women, and there are more men in the Conservative Party than in the Labour Party, this may not be a genuine association at all, but rather a sideshow of known gender differences across political parties. So how do we get to the bottom of this? A statistical manoeuvre called 'adjusting' the data that takes these confusing factors into account would sort things out for us.

But even where we discover an honest and straightforward link between two factors, we can't be sure what is causing what. For example, assuming that we have proved a real link between being a signed-up Conservative and having a satisfactory sex life, does being a Conservative render you more satisfied with your sex life, or do people who are more satisfied with their sex lives tend (for whatever reason) to become Conservatives?

One way to try to untangle 'causes' and 'effects' like these is to track the same individuals in long-term follow-up studies over prolonged periods of time. But where could you find researchers with the vision, patience and stamina to carry out this type of research? New Zealand would be a good place to start.

Tracking self-regard

If you were born in the city of Dunedin on the south island of New Zealand, you have good reason to feel lucky. If you happened to have been born there between 1 April 1972 and 31 March 1973, you might feel luckier still. No matter where in the world you happen to be living, you have been flown back to Dunedin, expenses paid, on frequent return trips. Fantastic.

Unless, that is, you happen to hate repeat physical examinations, dental assessments, countless blood tests, endless questionnaires and surveys, and being generally prodded, poked and scanned until you are driven witless. This is because the 1,037 people born over the course of 1972–3 were entered into the Dunedin Longitudinal Study, one of the best-known long-running 'cohort studies' in the world. It's certainly not one of the biggest, but because it had a staggering 96% early-retention rate, it is one of the most complete data sets available. And it has already yielded a rich harvest of knowledge about human growth and development.

The advantage of this kind of longitudinal study is that you can measure self-esteem at, say, age eleven, and then investigate how that links later to some of the claims on our 'fact' sheet, for example the risk of unwanted teenage pregnancy. Of course, even this wouldn't *conclusively* prove that low self-esteem is the cause, even though you have shown that it precedes the teenage pregnancy. But it does strengthen the case, especially if we can also use statistical tools to get rid of the effects of other possible risk factors (such as coming from a broken home). So, staying with teenage pregnancy, what did the Dunedin study show us about self-esteem and the risk of this and other issues, such as sexually transmitted diseases and drug misuse?

Sex, drugs and drinkers

The idea that low self-esteem and a consequent longing for love and affirmation lie at the root of teenage pregnancy seems so obvious to many folk that they have stopped thinking about it altogether. It's a 'fact' on the 'factsheet', so it must be true. The Dunedin long-term study revealed a different picture, however.

The researchers managed to get all their subjects to rate their self-esteem at age eleven.[9] Then, ten years later at age twenty-one, they asked them whether they had had sexual intercourse before the age of sixteen. They found *no* relationship between self-esteem at age eleven and early risky sexual behaviour. The researchers then carried out more sophisticated analyses to take into account all the possible confusing factors and they still couldn't find a link between low self-esteem and early sexual initiation.

Another long-term study in New Zealand illustrates just how important it is to make these kinds of careful statistical adjustments.[10] This particular group of researchers had a handy stack of self-esteem scores left over from a study carried out on a large group of fifteen-year-old teenagers many years earlier. So they looked into their sexual behaviour over the next ten years to see whether they could find a link with low self-esteem. Hey presto, those who reported low self-esteem at age fifteen also claimed a greater number of sexual partners, had an increased risk of unplanned pregnancies and reported less use of protection against sexually transmitted diseases, such as condoms.

But then the researchers did their sums again. Only this time they took into account differences among the youngsters, such as IQ, social class, history of child abuse and family instability. After adjusting for these factors, the link between self-esteem at fifteen and subsequent risky sexual behaviours all but disappeared. The research team concluded that the real link was between risky sexual behaviour and, say, coming from a broken home or having low IQ, rather than with self-esteem per se.

What about street drugs and alcohol abuse? Again, in many drug rehabilitation programmes it is almost an article of faith that, if you go looking for the root of the problem, you will find a shrivelled sense of self. So programmes try to 'address' the problem with self-affirming mantras such as, 'Today I will accept myself for who I am.' Website testimonials jostle to share the life-changing moment when 'I came to love and like myself for who I am'.

Now, as we saw earlier, people *do* need to accept themselves as a first step to taking responsibility and as part of the process of integration and ownership of life's problems. People *do* need to adopt a compassionate attitude towards themselves as part of a general act of self-governance and self-discipline in pursuit of some greater purpose. And we *are* built for love and for being loved. But is there hard evidence that making self-love and 'acceptance' the principle focus of your life actually does any good? Roy Baumeister found no evidence of a link between self-esteem and drug misuse, and Nicholas Emler came up with the same findings in Great Britain.[11]

Bully-boys and mobsters

The idea that low self-esteem is an important cause of aggression and anti-social behaviour is another knee-jerk assumption woven into our cultural zeitgeist:

> Sociopathic gangsters, despite their self-presentation as tough macho-men, are often driven by their deep feelings of low

self-esteem. This feeling of being a nobody is partially derived from the abuse and abandonment of their family. Because of this and other factors early in their life, they are constantly on a quest of proving their masculinity to compensate for their underlying low self-concept.[12]

So behind their tough exteriors, bullies and psychopaths harbour a seething world of self-doubt and insecurity. That's why they band together into gangs and boast of their exploits on Facebook. But what does the research actually show?

Once again, as for risky sexual behaviours and substance misuse, there is plenty of evidence of a link between growing up to be a bully-boy and having a deprived background, abusive parents or poor peer relationships. But it seems that 'low self-esteem' is a consequence of these background factors, rather than a causal factor in its own right. More importantly, neither Roy Baumeister nor Nicholas Emler could uncover convincing evidence that boosting self-esteem is useful in either the prevention or the 'cure' of these behavioural and social issues.

A recent study has questioned Baumeister and Emler's conclusions, on the basis of some new findings that suggest there may indeed be a weak link between self-esteem and certain aggressive behaviours, but even here researchers found that it was relatively small and hard to measure.[13] The same group of researchers have also recently published new findings from the Dunedin study[14] that suggest there is a link between low self-esteem and a range of outcomes, such as poor health, criminal behaviour and economic under-achievement. But although the researchers carry out careful adjustments when doing their sums, the links are weak and it's still not possible to conclude that low self-esteem really is the cause of these problems. At best, the jury is still out on this one.

The same raft of contradictory findings applies across the whole field of anti-social behaviours. Cheating among school-children, for example, appears to be associated with both low and high self-esteem. High-self-esteem kids were especially liable to cheat if their self-regard was linked with a need for approval.

Researchers have tried to explain contradictory findings like these by drawing a distinction between 'true' self-esteem and 'fragile' or 'defensive' self-esteem. The idea is that some people are simply putting on a front and it's the front that is being picked up by self-esteem questionnaires. The problem with these 'secret' or 'hidden' selves is that, almost by defin-ition, their existence is hard to disprove. Counsellors and psychoanalysts have thrived for years on this marketing ploy: if you don't accept their particular insight into the underlying, hidden 'cause' that only they can see, maybe it's because your secret self is resisting its discovery? Similarly, in self-esteem studies, if you can't find any evidence that bullies have low self-esteem, it's because, well, maybe it is 'hidden' out of sight. I am not saying that this isn't possible, just that it's hard to know either way.

Nicholas Emler makes another important point: rather than showing a link with low self-esteem, many studies suggest that violent and thuggish men often have an excess of self-belief and self-regard. In one study, for example, subjects were asked to administer painful blasts of noise to people who, they were told, were long-suffering volunteers in the next room; those with the highest form of self-regard called narcissism were more likely to administer painful blasts than other study participants.[15] A number of other studies have noticed a potential for callous and aggressive behaviour in men who like to look 'good (or gorgeous) in their own eyes'.[16] Of course, it may all come down to the fact that deep inside, they are really insecure little boys whose mothers didn't love them. This will certainly be true for some, but in general the evidence doesn't stack up that the self-esteem model itself gets us to the root of the problem.

Weighed in the balance

OK, it's time to be blunt. There is no hard evidence that self-esteem is a major cause of the list of social and psychological problems as has been claimed, and no proof that boosting self-esteem has any benefit in addressing these issues. The self-esteem project has been weighed in the balance and found wanting.

In fact, alarm bells should have been ringing at the very launch of the California Task Force on Self-Esteem way back in 1986.[17] The idea, remember, was that it was possible to 'inoculate' the population with self-esteem in order to protect them, much as a vaccine protects against physical disease. This was a 'social vaccine', and the enthusiasts of boosterism promised a raft of benefits and positive outcomes. Indeed, some advocates even argued that it might one day balance the state budget, because people with high self-esteem tend to pay more taxes!

The self-esteem project has been weighed in the balance and found wanting.

Around the same time a team of academics was commissioned to clarify the evidence base for this huge new initiative, and their conclusions make interesting reading. In the introduction to their final report published three years later, one of the authors makes this extraordinary admission: 'One of the disappointing aspects of *every chapter* [emphasis mine] in this volume . . . is how low the associations between self-esteem and its (presumed) consequences are in research to date.'[18]

The authors seem to be saying that claims about the benefits of self-esteem are justified, except for one small fly in the ointment: we don't have any proof. At this point, some academics pressed for the whole project to be placed on hold, pending further research. But self-esteem ideology had by now so ensconced itself in popular culture that few people out there seemed to care about the evidence anyway. And so, with the cultural wind blowing its way, the project sailed on, buoyed up by the uncritical enthusiasm and prestige of its academic backers. Self-esteem implementation committees were set up across the State, with the grand vision of a 'roll-out' across the nation. The Task Force report set the tone for a broader movement defined by the triumph of hope over reality and form over substance. And the rest, as they say, is history.

We have answered our first question: 'Does boosterism work?' with a resounding negative. But what about our second question? If not, does it do more harm than good?

6. THE AGE OF THE NARCISSIST

Repeating positive self-statements may benefit certain people,
but backfire for the very people who 'need' them the most.
'Positive Self-Statements: Power for Some,
Peril for Others', *Psychological Science*[1]

We would not want drugs to go to market that are essentially
untested and that have only their promoters' claims to back them
up. Yet we routinely rely on such claims to buy educational and
organizational products and services. People's lives may be affected
in much the same way as their lives can be affected by drugs . . .
Robert J. Sternberg, Yale University[2]

Being an unreconstructed hypochondriac, I'm a sucker for all
kinds of vitamins, health supplements and 'remedies', and it
turns out I'm not alone. A survey carried out in 2004[3] charted
the seemingly unstoppable rise of alternative medicines across
Western culture. As a quick flick through the lifestyle sections
of weekend newspapers will confirm, we are fascinated by
the latest thing in 'detox' programmes, or the supposed
benefits of a line of smooth hot stones balanced along our
spines, the energizing vibes of 'crystal therapy' and all the
other 'treatments' that fill the shelves of our local 'healing'

and 'health' shops. But what's the problem? All we lose is our money, right?

Health warning

Wrong. Alternative medicines have side-effects too. A recent Australian study uncovered a series of adverse events associated with the use of complementary medicines, including four reported deaths.[4] At best, they may simply delay, or divert, people from seeking expert advice. At worst, some come loaded with toxic side-effects of their own. So even if alternative remedies only 'work' because people believe that they work (the placebo effect), we need to be sure that the risks don't outweigh potential benefits. And that is true of 'mainstream' treatments and therapies too.

But do these kinds of health warnings apply only to physical treatments such as herbal remedies or diet supplements? Not so, according to Robert Sternberg of Yale University. We wouldn't allow drugs to go to market untested, with only their promoters' claims to back them up, he says, so why do we 'routinely rely on such claims to buy educational and organizational products and services? People's lives may be affected in much the same way as their lives can be affected by drugs . . .'[5] Playing around with somebody's state of mind isn't a risk-free operation. Psychological and educational interventions can have toxic side-effects too.

Loveable me

So what about efforts to boost self-esteem? How harmless are they? Researchers at the University of Waterloo in Ontario carried out a clever study[6] into the impact of repeating, mantra-style, familiar stock phrases, such as 'I'm a lovable person'; 'I'm powerful, I'm strong'; and 'Nothing in this world can stop me!' These techniques have been the bread and butter of the self-help movement since Norman Vincent Peale's *The Power of Positive Thinking* was first published back in 1952. Today millions of people go about their daily lives, silently repeating positive statements like these. The Ontario researchers found in fact that over 50% of survey respondents said that they 'frequently' use these kinds of self-affirmations; only 3% said that they 'never' use them.

Despite its popularity, the benefits (and risks) of this kind of self-help have not been properly established or researched. Previous studies haven't controlled for natural fluctuations in mood and subjective well-being, or they have ignored the general placebo effect that kicks in when we decide to do something about our lives. So the Ontario researchers decided to carry out their own series of experiments.

They persuaded a group of guinea-pig subjects to repeat and then to 'focus positively' on a range of positive self-statements, such as 'I'm a loveable person', and 'Nothing in the world can stop me'. Then their emotional responses were analysed alongside those of two comparison groups of subjects: the people in the first comparison group got the same statements but were asked to meditate on 'how this is both true and not true', while those in the other group were told to do nothing at all.

What did the researchers discover when they compared the three groups? Participants with low self-esteem at the start of the study actually felt *worse* after repeating and focusing positively on their self-affirming statements, compared with those in the other groups. In fact, repeating these stock phrases only had a good effect (although not by very much) on those already enjoying high self-esteem. The authors concluded that repeating positive self-statements may benefit certain people, but backfire for the very people who need them most.

We don't know for sure why making these kinds of positive statements causes people who already have low self-esteem to feel worse. One idea is that we all have a 'latitude of acceptance' towards ideas about ourselves that don't fit in with our self-image. In other words, we can fool ourselves some of the time, but not all of the time. Messages that fall outside our 'latitude of acceptance' may in fact boomerang, leading us to hold on to our original position even more strongly.[7] So we can all take a bit of 'spin' about our self-image, provided it doesn't err into complete fantasy. But repeating mantras, such as 'I am a magical/mystical/sparkling etc. person', when a quick glance in the mirror tells us otherwise, may do more harm than good.

Interestingly, the authors go on to suggest (although they don't have proof) that 'moderately' positive self-statements involving *specific strengths* (e.g. 'I am able to communicate well with young people'; 'I am a good Bible teacher') are less likely than *global* statements (e.g. 'I am a wonderful person') to provoke a rejection. In other words, as we shall see in a later chapter, affirming our strengths in *specific areas* may produce benefits in a way that global 'I-am-special' statements do not. Let's hang on to that thought for later.

Narcissism and entitlement

So how might the boosterism project of the last quarter-century have backfired on us?

In a much-watched YouTube video of the British television programme *The X Factor*, a young man called Robert strides onto the stage with an air of studied seriousness. He tells the judges that he 'works in a chicken factory'. What follows is a pantomime effort of screeching falsetto, honed apparently in local karaoke bars. In reply to the frosty response from the judges, Robert reassures them that when he sings in bars he 'gets applause' and 'it's genuine'. Simon Cowell levels with him in customary style: 'Robert, I can honestly say you are the worst singer I have ever heard in my life.' 'Thank you,' replies Robert with a look of genuine sincerity. Robert appears to lack self-awareness to such a degree that he even interprets negative feedback as being some kind of compliment.[8]

In another *X Factor* audition, the one voted in 2007 by Simon Cowell as the 'worst ever', a young woman ('all of Cardiff know me') announces that she is 'a natural raw talent . . . At the end of the day I deserve it . . . I'm just too [darned] good.' After the delivery of a, shall we say, less-than-average performance, she announces to the judges, 'That was good, wasn't it?' When she doesn't get the acclaim she expects, she reacts venomously and, as her behaviour escalates, eventually needs to be escorted from the building by one of the bouncers.[9]

Now I have serious concerns about the 'peep-show' dynamics that operate in programmes like *American Idol* and *The X Factor*. There's a risk that television producers, anxious to provide entertainment fodder for the amusement of baying television audiences, may well filter in vulnerable young people. The result is that these programmes become a modern equivalent of the fairground freak shows of the past, with their parades of bearded ladies, dwarves and elephant men. The only difference is that marginal conditions are now played out more subtly for our amusement by those with unusual personalities. No matter how much we may applaud the 'fearless honesty' of the judges (really?), or believe that puncturing people's prideful defences serves a useful social function, the blatant pleasure taken in such ritual humiliation raises serious questions.

But whatever the rights and wrongs of these shows, the critical question is how far such self-serving and self-deluded behaviour paraded on our television screens is simply the tip of an iceberg? Is it possible that these cameo performances are just extreme examples of a more general narcissism phenomenon spread across the population? In other words, just as increasing problems with alcohol addiction reflect a rise in the consumption of alcohol in the whole population more generally, do the celebrity-hungry, entitled and narcissistic kids who offer themselves on our TV screens represent the thin end of the wedge of a broader cultural change that affects us all? Most of us have sufficient self-awareness to avoid getting ourselves onto programmes like *The X Factor*, but how much of our own behaviour is being fuelled by a comparable sense of 'entitlement', and driven by a similar hunger for recognition and acclaim?

In 2008 academics at the University of Wyoming, USA read about Jean Twenge's work on entitlement and decided to conduct a local survey of their own.[10] Did her research findings hold up among their local students? They found that 92% of them agreed with the statement, 'I am an intelligent person'; 88% agreed with, 'I want to be able to reflect on life later and say I followed my dreams'; and a whopping 61% agreed with, 'It's important that I come first on my list of priorities.' So we shouldn't be surprised to learn then that practically the whole sample – 95% – agreed with the statement, 'I take a positive attitude towards myself.' After all, in today's climate, to do otherwise would be a cardinal sin.

Besides their inflated view of themselves, students nurtured huge expectations of the future too: 92% agreed with the statement, 'I will get to where I want in life someday'; 53% of students responded that they had difficulty in accepting criticism; and, when asked how they liked to receive criticism, nearly 70% said that they like 'to be complimented first, and then given suggestions'.

Responses by faculty staff were consistent with the general pattern: over 50% had experienced a student arguing for a higher grade at least 'occasionally' during the semester, and nearly 1 in 6 said they had experienced this 'many times'. After all, 38% of the students had agreed with the statement, 'College is like a business; I am paying for a degree and expect to receive one.' Staff commented upon the prevailing 'customer-is-always-right' attitudes among pupils, and 70% indicated that they were 'occasionally or often' surprised by inappropriate informality in communications. One student emailed a staff member, 'Hiya Smith, can you tell me what I got in the exam? When are you going to post the grades? PS – I won't be in class tomorrow, so can I get the notes?' Another messaged, 'Hey Steph! Yes, I need an extension on that paper; I'm sure you won't mind!' One teacher was contacted, 'Dude, I'm failing your class. What am I supposed to do?'

This is the price we now pay for half a century of self-esteem and over three decades of boosterism. The self-esteem project has backfired spectacularly. Many social commentators agree. They have identified a new 'culture of narcissism',[11] a new 'generation Me'[12] that is both the product of, and a continuing dynamo for, our preoccupations with how much we are 'worth'. But has there been a *real and measurable* rise in these more extreme narcissistic behaviours in recent years? And if so, can we really blame that on the efforts of the self-esteem industries?

The low-down on high self-regard

Let's return to the work of the psychologist Jean Twenge. Twenge has explored trends in narcissism-related attitudes, using a psychological tool called the Narcissistic Personality Inventory (NPI). Narcissists who score highly on the NPI tend to have an inflated sense of self-importance and grandiosity. They feel superior to other people, court attention and manipulate situations towards their ends. Narcissists lack empathy to such a degree that they are genuinely shocked and dismayed when the admiration and praise they expect isn't forthcoming. But because of their lack of self-awareness, they quickly bounce back to continue in their own sweet way, dousing themselves with fantasies of success, power and brilliance. Coddling a sense of entitlement, narcissists expect that they will always be pandered to and blithely assume that they top the list of everybody else's concerns. Displaying priggish, patronizing and disdainful reactions to the achievements of others, arrogant and haughty behaviour is pretty much the rule.

Do you recognize yourself here? You may well have caught a glimpse of yourself in this description, because personality characteristics tend to lie on a spectrum and fade into one another. But when these traits colonize a personality to the extent that they are pervasive and dominating, psychologists talk about the 'narcissistic personality'. Sometimes these traits are so severe that they disrupt relationships and lead to severe distress (usually in other people!), or they hamper a person's ability to function socially and earn a living. In such cases, psychiatrists talk about the individual having a 'Narcissistic Personality Disorder'. When we want to measure these kinds of personality types in the general population, the NPI, which asks individuals whether they endorse statements such as, 'I think I'm a special person'; 'I can live my life any way I want to'; or 'If I ruled the world, it would be a better place', is still one of the most popular measurement tools in this whole area.

Twenge and colleagues[13] analysed responses to the NPI among 15,234 college students, collected between 1987 and 2006. What did they discover? Over the nineteen years there had been a marked increase in narcissism generally, with the most recently recruited students appearing significantly more narcissistic. In fact, the average student in 2006 scored higher than 65% of students in 1987. Not everybody agrees with Twenge's conclusions, but the data mirrors the findings of many other researchers too. For example, as we saw earlier, Newsome and colleagues[14] found that in the early 1950s only 12% of teens aged fourteen to sixteen agreed with the statement, 'I am an important person', but by the late 1980s 80% claimed to feel important in this way. Lillian Katz of the University of Illinois also believes that having fixated on boosting young people's self-esteem for so long, we have unthinkingly built a generation of narcissists.[15]

Twenge also points to studies that show how narcissists tend to lash out aggressively when they are insulted or rejected. She wonders whether incidents such as the tragic shootings at Columbine High School in the USA reflected severe narcissistic traits in the personalities of the young men who were responsible for the deaths of so many innocent people.[16] This is conjecture of course, but there is some evidence for her case. Narcissistic men, for example, show less feeling for, and understanding of, the plight of rape victims.[17]

There are a number of problems in accepting these types of tracking data at face value, however, and we need to be cautious about jumping to conclusions about the state of mind of 'young people today'. First, there is an inevitable degree of 'data picking' and 'evidence selection' when we attempt to characterize broad social trends and then identify the culprits. Also, more specifically, the social profile of college students changed dramatically between 1965 and 2000, with an inflow of students from poorer backgrounds and ethnic minorities. There have also been changes in the relative proportions of men and women. Twenge is a careful researcher, however, who attempted to take these factors into account in her analyses. And she argues that changes in the social and ethnic make-up of students have been much less than we might imagine, in the United States at least, citing data that the median income of college students' parents, when adjusted for inflation, did not change dramatically between 1965 and 2000.

But perhaps the changes Twenge reports simply reflect a greater willingness to admit to problems among younger people in recent generations? Maybe they are simply willing to be more honest about themselves? Twenge looked into this, however, and found that changes in responses to the NPI and other scales seemed to be occurring independently of people's willingness to talk about themselves honestly. So these points go some way to reassuring Twenge's critics, and it does indeed appear that narcissism is really on the increase. But we need to be careful.

Generation glum?

There is another area in which the self-esteem movement may have backfired on us, seen in increasing rates of depression and anxiety. In Britain a large-scale survey of 16–25-year-olds carried out in 2008 gave an alarming insight into today's 'unhappy younger generation'.[18] More than 1 in 10 (12%) said that life was meaningless; more than a quarter (27%) admitted they were 'often' or 'always' down or depressed; greater than a quarter (29%) of young men and women said they are less happy now than they had been as a child, and 1 in 5 felt like crying 'often' or 'always'. Almost half (47%) said they were regularly stressed.

So has the self-esteem movement produced a generation of unhappy twenty- and thirty-somethings? There are plausible reasons for thinking that this might be the case. The Tyler Durden character in the film *Fight Club* was onto something when he said, 'Our generation has had no Great Depression, no Great War. Depression is our lives . . . We were raised on television to believe that we'd all be millionaires, movie gods, rock stars, but we won't. And we're starting to figure that out.'

Those born after 1970 have had their expectations raised way beyond anything experienced in any previous generation. They have been duped into believing that 'you can have it all'. The snaking lines of kids waiting for their *American Idol* or *The X Factor* auditions bear witness to the hopes and aspirations of a generation that believes in its own brand of specialness. By the age of eighteen the average teenager has absorbed literally thousands of advertisements and messages selling the idea that what they now have (trainers, make-up, iPhone 3, iPad 2) is just plain old second-rate – they are entitled to something better. Why? 'Because you're worth it!'

In such a culture of entitlement is it surprising then that, when expectations hit the buffers of reality and dreams turn to dust, so many young people report high levels of depression, gloom and anxiety? The all-out narcissist doesn't care about reality of course – their lack of self-awareness and empathy allows them to go their own sweet way, unhindered by the inconveniences of the truth about their personality and behaviour. But for the vast majority of young people, still sensitive to the opinions of others and desperate for approval, their failure to hit the big time may be leading them to hit out – not at others, but themselves.

Convinced by the argument? It sounds plausible. But is there enough hard evidence to prove conclusively that there have been big rises in actual psychiatric disorders such as depressive illness in recent years and that the self-esteem movement is the culprit? In one of her books, Jean Twenge marshals considerable evidence to show that anxiety, depression, suicidal behaviours and the use of medication have all increased markedly in recent decades. Her data suggest that the risk of suffering a major depression is 'ten times higher' compared with only last century.[19] Is she right? On this count I am not so sure.

Claims like this get us into murky and difficult waters. There are conflicting findings in this area, and when we are thinking about psychiatric disorders (as opposed to more general feelings described in questionnaires), we have to be careful before accepting assertions at face value.[20, 21] Not all claims are based upon the comparison of 'like-for-like' instruments, and errors can creep in, depending on where a particular question is placed in the interview. Also, just because respondents report a particular symptom does not mean they suffer a full-blown disorder, and yet many commentators are happy to jump from one to the other. And as more information about depression and anxiety becomes available on the internet and stigma attitudes begin to soften, individuals may simply be more ready to talk about their problems.

Finally, even if there has been such a specific rise, remember that correlation does not prove causation. There are numerous culprits besides the self-esteem movement, including increased family instability, different social support patterns, the sexualization of culture, with accompanying relationship instability, and increased substance misuse.

So what can we conclude?

If you are feeling frustrated at this point, please bear with me. Sometimes it can feel as though psychiatrists and psychologists are rehearsing the blindingly obvious or getting themselves entangled in the hopelessly obscure. But we shouldn't be too surprised. Human beings, made in the image of God, will always confound the reductionist assertions and confident predictions of social scientists. We have to do the best we can, stand back from the evidence and, as objectively as we are able, arrive at a balanced conclusion.

So what can we safely conclude about the negative impact of the boosterism movement? First, surveys show that over the past three decades people have been more ready to endorse statements of self-importance, entitlement and other traits of narcissism. The evidence here is pretty conclusive. Secondly, it is *likely* that the self-esteem movement has contributed significantly to the rise of narcissism and Narcissistic Personality Disorders, but we can't be absolutely sure that 'boosterism' is the sole culprit. Both phenomena may be related to something else. We mustn't fall into the trap of assuming that correlation is the same thing as causation, especially when we have taken such a hard line against those who do.

Not everybody will agree with these first two conclusions. For example, Twenge cites a large number of anecdotes and surveys that portray the behaviour of 'generation Me' (which she defines as those born in the 1970s, 1980s and 1990s) as being often socially feckless, disrespectful, rude, opinionated and lacking empathy. Authors such as Neil Howe and William Strauss, however, who researched what they call the 'Millennial Generation' (those born in the later years of that period, the 1980s and 1990s), argue that young people born towards the end of the period have markedly *more* regard for one another, their communities and their parents. They point out that, since 1994, violent crime has actually fallen among under-twenty-fives in the United States, and there is evidence that post-millennial young adults continue to have strong family values and to participate in volunteering.[22]

Despite these conflicting data, in my view the weight of the evidence leans towards Twenge's conclusions. It is likely that the self-esteem movement has been a substantial factor in several unfortunate social trends, and especially the rise of narcissism and entitlement.

Thirdly and finally, the self-esteem movement *may* be associated with a rise in unhappiness and discontentment among young adults, but here we can't be sure. There are plausible reasons for linking the two, not least the work about 'positive self-statements' we reviewed at the beginning of this chapter, but so far the jury is still out on this one.

we need a stronger, more durable way of thinking about ourselves.

Overall, from our survey of the data, I believe we can be sure that boosterism has done us no good, and there's a strong suspicion that it has actually caused harm. It's time to go back to the drawing board. We need a stronger, more durable way of thinking about ourselves. But before we go looking, there is one more area in which the self-esteem movement promised big and delivered small. We turn now to explore the way in which it has shaped and transformed the education of our children.

7. KIDS PRAISE

The story the children are about to hear tells of some of the
animals that live in the forest. Of all the animals, it is Mouse who
has forgotten that she has her own special gift. The children are
going to try and help Mouse to believe in herself. Every time Mouse
*says, '**I'm no good; I'm only a mouse**,' some of the children are*
*going to whisper: '**Believe in yourself; believe in yourself**,'*
several times to help her to remember that it is good to be who
she is . . . before they leave, ask the children and adults to
whisper out loud 'It's good to be me.'
Guidance material for running a school assembly,
from UK Government national strategy for 'Social and
Emotional Aspects of Learning' (SEAL)

Far from creating a more balanced and rounded personality,
therapeutic education promotes . . . a life focused on self-fulfilment
rather than with understanding and changing the world.
The paradox of therapeutic education . . . is that you will not
change the world and nor will you change yourself.
Kathryn Ecclestone and Dennis Hayes[1]

Remember the pass-the-parcel scenario at the beginning of
this book? When I was a kid there was only one winner and

one prize. Now, five decades later, the game seems to have mutated through some big changes. For a start, there is a prize under nearly every layer of wrapping paper. And, mysteriously, the timing of the 'random' pauses in the music is so strategic and deliberate that, by the end of the game, every child is found to be clutching an identical prize. And why does everybody need to win? Because we don't want to erode the kids' self-esteem.

The idea that high self-esteem is the key to healthy childhood development is all around us. Those who dare to raise questions and come out with doubts are portrayed as knuckle-draggers stuck in the past, or kill-joys who just don't like to see people being happy. And because the issue of low self-esteem in young women has been such an important plank of the feminist agenda, sympathetic social commentators have been reluctant to appear to be taking shots at their own side too.

In parenting and education, as elsewhere, the self-esteem agenda has achieved the status of 'no-brainer'. Nicholas Emler notes,

> Because [we all assumed] self-esteem is both desirable for society as a whole and the right of every individual, all practices or circumstances that could conceivably damage a person's self-esteem were to be purged from the curriculum of life (and certainly from the precincts of educational establishments). Any reluctance to pursue this agenda could be attacked with all the self-righteous moral certainty of a lynching party.[2]

Parenting a princess

So how has self-esteem ideology affected modern parenting? Could the roots of narcissism be blamed on the changed attitudes towards childcare and discipline over the last few decades?

It has never been easy being a mum or a dad. Kids are hard work. I remember first hearing the cry of one of my grandsons a few hours after he had emerged into the blinding glare of the maternity unit. I recall thinking how that cry, that reflex, instinctive rush of breath through tightened vocal cords was the only means he had, the only tool he possessed, to attract his mother's attention and ensure that his wants and needs would be met. And then I smiled as I reflected on how he would use that tool to such good effect over the next few years: *I want, I need and I will have NOW!* Whether we pin the blame on the raw power of the id, or prefer to underscore the biblical doctrine of original sin, it has never been easy for parents to say 'no'.

And it's a lot harder in a culture of entitlement. Our shopping habits dangle temptation before our children's eyes. Think running the gauntlet of the supermarket checkout, fumbling for your credit card while surrounded by shelves of sweets set strategically in the sightline of your toddler. And our kids don't have to wait any more to go down to the shops to encounter choice and opportunity. Page after page of product information is beamed to their TVs, computers, mobiles and social media accounts. I had tea recently with the headmaster of a famous English public school who lamented how, despite the refined and highly controlled social environment that his school provided, he found himself increasingly helpless in the face of social media's ability to pole-vault above his head and directly into the hearts and minds of his pupils. He was especially concerned about the way kids could be seduced as 'product champions', motivated to market goods and services through their social media friends and contacts. Advertising, product placement and social media have forged a powerful alliance to wear down parental resistance.

It's even harder to say 'no' in a culture in which self-esteem is viewed as being so important and yet so perilously fragile. Good parents don't want to put the health, wealth, educational achievement and personality development of their kids at risk by precipitating a downward spiral of self-esteem. So we overpraise, overprotect and give in to their demands. Because failure is another way of experiencing life's 'no', we try to shield children against its reality too, either by avoiding competition altogether or by cushioning them against life's unfairness. As far as we can, we make sure there are no losers and that everybody gets a prize.

My grandson has made a good start in this department already. Just eighteen months old, he returned from his nursery sports day, brandishing a 'certificate of participation'. You get a commendation just for turning up. He isn't yet wearing a Prince Charming T-shirt, but I suspect it's on its way. It's notable how a significant proportion of kids' T-shirts now sport royal labels such as 'Princess'. You can upgrade to 'Unique Princess', 'Cool Princess' and 'Pink Princess' if you like or, depending on where you live, opt for something more personal like 'Princess of Kazakhstan'. I saw one recently that was branded, 'It's all about ME, only Me, just Me, all Me!' So no room for doubt there.

Being a Christian confers a definite advantage in the self-image T-shirt stakes. I've spotted one labelled (in very bold letters), 'Yes I am a Princess', followed (in rather small letters) by 'My Father is the King of Kings!' How's that for an upgrade? Indeed, if you desire, the whole counsel of God can be plundered to relaunch your self-brand: I've seen kids wearing 'In God's Eyes I'm So Cool! God's Little Masterpiece!' And perhaps the best one of all: 'When God Made Me He Was Just Showing Off!' How can the world compete with that?

But as Twenge and Campbell observe in *The Narcissism Epidemic*, 'If your daughter is a princess, does this mean that you are queen or king? No – it means you are the loyal subject, and you must do what the princess says.'[3] They cite supportive data from a nationwide survey that asked parents to choose and then rank the top five things a child needed to prepare him (or her) for life: 'Back in 1958 . . . people said that the second most important thing a child could learn was "to obey". Not any more. Throughout the 1980s and '90s the importance of obedience steadily declined until it was ranked second to last [and] reached an all-time low in 2004, the last year for which data are available.'[4]

These kinds of data confirm popular suspicions that modern parents preside over an atmosphere of too much praise, too little failure and insufficient boundary-setting, leaving many young people ill-equipped for the harsh realities of life. And when we award them T-shirts that say, 'Future reality show contestant', we shouldn't be surprised when this turns out to be their only ambition.

Of course, few parents set out to create narcissists or produce vulnerable, self-absorbed young people who lack resilience. We simply want the best for our children. I am certainly not arguing for a blanket return to some of the harsh and unprincipled disciplines of the past. I recall, as a quarrelling child, being smacked (very gently – it was the ignominy that hurt) even though my mother couldn't be sure which one of us was to blame. When I protested that such indiscriminate retribution was patently unfair, she would reply that life isn't fair, and that was that. It's not a bad lesson actually, but I don't think we would want to reinstate that approach to childcare. But have we, in thrall to self-esteem ideology, overbalanced too far in the opposite direction? I think we have.

Teacher's pet

In chapter 5 we explored the huge impact of the self-esteem movement in the world of education, and here too we are witnessing growing concern about its harmful effects on child development and emotional resilience. Take the UK Government's SEAL initiative introduced once again in our 'mouse' scenario at the start of this chapter. Launched in 2005, SEAL seeks to enhance the emotional and personal development of children across the entire educational spectrum.

On the face of it, it is hard to argue with many of the goals that SEAL sets out to achieve. Who could disagree, for example, that children should be able to affirm the statement: 'I understand that changing the way I think about people and events changes the way I feel about them.' Or that secondary school children should be able to assert, 'I can make sense of what has happened to me in my life and understand that things that come from my own history can make me feel prone to being upset or angry, for reasons that others may find it difficult to understand', even if it is a bit of mouthful? But several commentators highlight potential pitfalls in SEAL and similar programmes, and we should share their concerns.

For a start, Carol Craig of the Scottish Centre for Confidence questions the robustness of the evidence base supporting such a huge and systematic intervention in the hearts and minds of a nation's young people: 'Formally teaching children from three to eighteen about their emotions or how to calm themselves, for example, has never been done before in the systematic way, year on year, that SEAL suggests. We have no idea whether this will be beneficial or not.'[5] Craig isn't against the broad aims of paying more attention to school ethos, helping support young people in building better relationships, eradicating bullying, and so on. But she is rightly concerned about the scope and scale of this nationwide initiative. And we should be concerned that, feeling discouraged and undermined by the emotional 'experts' at school, parents might shuffle off even further their responsibilities for the character development of their own children.

The second concern is that educational initiatives such as SEAL don't pay sufficient attention to the potential side-effects we talked about in the previous chapter. It is an extension of therapy culture, way beyond medicine, psychology and social services. Professor Kathryn Ecclestone, an educationalist at Oxford Brookes University, thinks there is a real danger that encouraging children to obsess about 'how I feel just now' risks turning children, young people and adults into anxious and self-preoccupied individuals, with lives 'focused on self-fulfilment rather than with understanding and changing the world'.[6] SEAL also seems to assume that expressing feelings is always 'a good thing'. But it was the same sentiment that underpinned the widespread implementation of 'psychological debriefing' of those caught up in disasters, before proper research showed it to be totally ineffective in the prevention of post-traumatic stress disorder.[7]

The third and perhaps most important area of concern is that, however nuanced and balanced the SEAL project may appear in promoting the broader emotional well-being of children, self-esteem and boosterism will inevitably attract the most attention because of their grip on culture more generally. The only comparable attempt on a national scale systematically to change the hearts and minds of young people has been the American schools' self-esteem movement,[8] and Craig is rightly worried that therapeutic education in Great Britain will simply suck everybody into the same self-esteem vortex.

As with other claims about its supposed beneficial effects, there is no evidence of there being a positive relationship between boosting self-esteem and subsequent educational achievement. There is certainly a *correlation* between the two: numerous studies show that self-esteem and educational attainment are linked. But even here the relationship isn't particularly strong; after examining around 300 such studies, one researcher estimated the strength of the correlation to be 0.16 (a perfect 'one-to-one' correlation would be 1.0).[9] For those interested in the technical side of things, a correlation of 0.16 is very, very low.

And even if the association were stronger, as we have seen, correlation doesn't prove causation. The 1970 British Cohort Study showed that self-esteem scores at age ten were only marginally related to later educational attainment.[10] In fact, studies suggest that children with low self-esteem try just as hard to succeed as those with high self-esteem. Their motivations and expectations may be different but the effect is pretty much the same.

The final concern about therapeutic education is the way in which resilience and competitive robustness among children are undermined. Because self-esteem is said to be so fragile, teachers, like parents, have become increasingly averse to exposing their pupils to anything that might damage it. With something as precious and (apparently) far-reaching in its consequences as a child's fragile self-esteem, genuine criticism has become far too risky, they suppose. Thus, a phoney egalitarianism gets institutionalized in schools, with teachers reluctant to voice relative judgments about their pupils. Standards get dumbed down and every ego requires a certificate of merit just for turning up. The logic is impeccable: children need to develop good self-esteem; self-esteem depends on praise and success; so 'all must have prizes'.[11]

Kids praise

But how should we give praise and encouragement? No parent or teacher thinks, 'I wonder what I can do today to destroy my child's confidence, rubbish their achievements and mock their efforts to do better.' We want our kids to flourish and be successful. So we dole out generous heaps of praise to try to get the best out of them. Children love to be praised too, and they absorb praise for their talents and cleverness like blotting paper. They like the 'you-are-brilliant/smart/special, etc.' endorsements best. It gives them a real shot in the arm.

However, when we overpraise children with global statements like these or, worse, allow them to overhear us picking off other people's children along the same lines ('What a thickhead that kid is'; 'She's a born winner'), we are sending them a dangerous message. We are teaching them that ability is a 'fixed' characteristic that you've either got or you haven't got.

Kids who have been taught this type of 'fixed' mindset are often *frightened* to fail, because, if success means you are smart, then failure means you are dumb. So they avoid challenges and resent negative feedback. Some of the most academically robust work in this area has been carried out by Professor Carol Dweck,[12] a long-time critic of the 'you're special' approach. It's all about *mindset*, she says.[13]

The word 'mindset' describes our basic psychological 'stance': the lens through which we look at the world. Are you a 'glass-half-empty' person? If so, then you have a broadly pessimistic, 'see-the-problems-wherever-possible' mindset that negates the positive side of the equation. Our mindset influences what we see, how we interpret it and, crucially, how we respond to the world.

As children develop, the numerous ways in which we interact with them, encouraging them here, discouraging them there, quietly construct a mindset that will stay with them for the rest of their lives. So, says Dweck, we need to pay attention to the messages we send when we say things like, 'You learnt that so quickly; you're clever!'; 'Wow, just look at those sums! We have among us, ladies and gentleman, Einstein in the making!'; 'Just look at that painting; Is this the next Michelangelo or what?' When we talk like this, what our children hear is, 'If I don't learn this quickly, I'm not clever; I'm a thickhead!'; 'If I don't get 100% next time round, I won't be like Einstein, so I'd better not attempt anything too hard'; 'If it goes wrong that won't be very special! So better just keep things simple . . . '

I once attended a conference in the Swiss Alps and stayed on for a couple of days' skiing. I was lucky to have there a group of about seven or eight friends with whom I'd skied after previous conferences. We pretty much knew one another's 'level' and could get ourselves round the mountains at about the same rate. Allowing for the occasional mini-disaster, our dignity was generally preserved and our egos left intact.

One afternoon we were taking a well-earned rest at the head of a new run, when a very keen-looking group of experts gracefully zigzagged their way through the deep virgin powder above us and came to a rest alongside. I recognized a good friend of mine among them, along with several other conference attendees. 'Hey, come and join us, Glynn,' my friend said. 'We've got a guide and we're heading off-piste.' I thought for half a micro-second before politely declining his offer. As the élite skiers went on their way, a member of our group observed, 'Glynn would rather be the best in this group than Mr Average in that . . . ' Ouch.

He was right. And something similar happens when we induce what Dweck calls 'fixed' mindsets in our children about being 'special', 'intelligent' and 'smart'. It encourages them to avoid challenges that might compromise the view they have formed about their abilities, and where they 'fit' into the scheme of things.

Dweck believes this approach has produced a generation of young people with fixed mindsets who can't get through the day without an award, and who expect success because they are special, not because they've worked hard. Kids like this tend to avoid opportunities to learn, in case they may make mistakes and, when they do make mistakes, rather than correct them, they will often try to hide them.[14] They don't believe they have to make the effort either, believing that ability comes with success guaranteed. 'This is one of the worst beliefs that students can hold,' concludes Dweck.

Dweck has validated her findings with some fascinating studies. In one of them she set a group of pupils a fairly easy task and then coached their teachers to praise half of them for their intrinsic ability ('You must be smart at these problems, brilliant'), and the other half for their efforts ('You must have worked hard at these problems, well done'). Dweck's team then asked the subjects to agree or disagree with statements such as: 'Your intelligence is something basic about you that can't really change' or 'You are either smart or you're not; you've got it or you haven't.'

Students who had been praised for their intelligence in a 'you've-got-natural-ability' sort of way were much more likely to agree with the fixed-mindset statements, in contrast to children praised for the effort they had put in. Similarly, children praised for their intelligence, when asked to define what they meant by intelligence, described it in terms of inflexible ability, whereas those praised for effort focused on skills and knowledge and the need to keep learning. In other words, when we praise ability, we strengthen fixed mindsets, but praising effort promotes 'growth' mindsets. So it's this 'growth mindset' that we need to be encouraging in our children.

But here's the compelling part of this research. The students were now offered a challenging task that would teach them some new skills or a dead-easy task that would guarantee a near perfect mark. The students who had been praised for effort – those cultivating a 'growth mindset' – sought out opportunities to learn and plumped for the more challenging tasks. Most of those praised for their intrinsic intelligence and ability, on the other hand, opted for the easy task. And in subsequent studies Dweck showed that students praised for effort were much more likely to persevere, whereas, when asked to anonymously report their final scores, almost 40% of those who had been praised for their intrinsic ability *lied* to the researchers.

The bottom line of these kinds of experiment is that Dweck advocates giving our children and students 'process' praise, rather than 'ability' or 'status' praise. Process praising highlights engagement, strategizing and persevering. You shift the focus from who they are to what they do: 'You really studied for your test, and your improvement shows it. Great – keep going'; 'You read the material over, then tested yourself on it. That really worked! Well done'; 'I like the way you tried all kinds of strategies until you finally got it.' For students who get it without even trying, Dweck says, 'All right, that was too easy for you; let's now do something more challenging that you can really learn from.'

But what about children who work hard and still don't do well? Say something such as, 'I like the effort you put in. Let's work together to try to figure out what you don't understand.' Or alternatively, you can try something like, 'We all learn at different speeds. It may take more time for you to catch on to this, but if you keep working at it, you will.'

Of course, it isn't easy to disentangle process from ability entirely. At some point a student has to come to terms with the 'fit' between her particular strengths and the task in hand. But the point is that praise and admiration are focused on the effort, not the individual. Kids shouldn't necessarily believe that anyone can become an Einstein or a Usain Bolt, but they should believe that even they had to put in years of effort and hard work to become who they were.[15]

Teaching a child how to cope with failure is crucial. When nine-year-old Melanie comes running in tears, devastated that she didn't even make the top three in the music competition, we don't do her any favours by telling her, 'Of course, we all thought you were the best', or 'Well, never mind, you are sure to win next time round.' Melanie needs to know that, if she wants to make it to the top position, clearly a lot more effort is going to be required – and if she isn't up for that, then why not just think about doing it for fun? We need to sympathize with her disappointment and ensure that nothing would ever lead her to suspect that somehow our love, support and acceptance of her is contingent on such performances. But she needs to learn to fail well. Giving her a phoney boost now will only lead to more disappointment further down the line.

Parent power

We have focused in this chapter on the crucial role that teachers and parents play in developing the way we think about ourselves and our abilities. Education is important, as we have seen. But in his review, Nicholas Emler shows just how important *parents* are for developing a confident self-concept. For example, ethnicity, social class and, surprisingly, gender have relatively weak or negligible effects. Even more surprising, our appearance and experiences of success or failure have only moderate effects. The two factors that have significant, or substantial, effects on the cultivation of a confident self-concept are genetics and the behaviour of parents.

Even through adolescence, when peer approval becomes more significant, parents' opinions remain significant well into adult life. So strong is this relationship that Emler is able to conclude, 'After parents and beyond mid-adolescents, no one else seems to achieve the same level of influence . . . It is almost as if, after parents have had their say – and their genetic influence – we become increasingly deaf to other, especially dissenting, voices.'[16] So parents matter a great deal. And how we praise and encourage our children is far too important to be left to the ineffective and potentially harmful advice offered by some experts of boosterism and self-esteem.

8. ALL ROADS LEAD TO PHILOSOPHY

'When I use a word,' Humpty Dumpty said,
in rather a scornful tone,
'it means just what I choose it to mean –
neither more nor less.'
Alice in Wonderland

There's a story going round that everything on Wikipedia connects to the page on philosophy. Go to the Wikipedia site and choose any word (such as 'apple'). Now research its meaning by clicking the first 'link' on the page (the first word in the body of the text, not pronunciation, derivation, etc.). Keep on clicking the meaning of each new word, and, sooner or later, you end up at the page for 'philosophy'. The first link for 'apple', for example, is 'pomaceous', so click on that. Keep repeating the process with each new word link and, hey presto, you arrive at 'philosophy'. I can't be sure it always works, but with 'apple' it took about seventeen clicks. All roads, you see, lead to philosophy.

With self-esteem it took just eleven clicks. And sure enough, as we near the end of our journey through the world of self-esteem, this particular road leads to philosophy as well. In fact, if we look around us, we discover that we are sitting in the middle of a philosophical and conceptual minefield. So we'd better watch where we step.

The definitions muddle

To start with, we find ourselves in a muddle about what the concept of 'self-esteem' actually means. Let me give three examples. Picture a young woman edging into a room among some party revellers, but then, flustered and embarrassed, slipping self-consciously out again. 'Big self-esteem issues,' you whisper to a friend. Or imagine a factory supervisor blowing up at a young novice apprentice. 'Five foot six inches, thirty-two years old and bald as a badger . . . fragile self-esteem – that's why he's so tetchy . . . ' you overhear somebody say. A student refuses to take part in a residence committee husting (or 'stump' as they say in the US), despite being the best person for the job. 'Come on, you could do it if you tried!' you encourage her, 'But you've got some work to do on your self-esteem!' From the way the term 'self-esteem' gets bandied about, you would think we all knew exactly what we were talking about.

But let's try this exercise. You choose twenty-five university undergraduates and invite them to join you for a drink after supper. After breaking them into groups, you ask them to write down what they mean when they use the term 'self-esteem'.[1] Sifting through the responses, the range and variety surprise you. On the face of it, everybody seems to think self-esteem is something to do with the way we 'look at' or 'think about' ourselves. So far so good.

But then you take a closer look at what's been written. Half of them talk about low self-esteem as a feeling rather than a thought. The sort of feeling you get when you walk self-consciously into a room and sense that people have been talking about you; or the haunting malaise that somehow you don't belong here and are about to be found out as an imposter. These students write about a 'deep-down feeling' that stalks like a mysterious, vaguely threatening stranger: 'You can't especially put it into words, but somehow you just "feel" that you are "no good".'

Others, however, see self-esteem as a way of thinking, not feeling. It's about 'taking a positive view of yourself' or 'believing that you are worthy of being happy' and that you have the 'ability to make a solid contribution to life'. Another group of students prefers to focus on behaviour, talking about self-esteem in terms of 'acting confidently', being 'assertive' or 'not letting people push you around'. It turns out that, as you review their responses, although we all talk about the term as though we all know what it means, we've stumbled across quite a range of definitions and approaches to the way it actually gets used.

Now you invite the students into a plenary discussion and ask them to think about the causes of self-esteem. Here we discover even more disagreement. Some think that 'good' self-esteem results from 'living well' and achieving your goals in life, the good feeling that comes when there is a sense of 'fit' between the opportunities that life offers and your ability to rise to them. As far as this section of opinion is concerned, self-esteem is something to do with 'confidence' and being recognized as competent and effective by your peers.

Others disagree. For them, healthy self-esteem radiates from somewhere deep in your psyche, a way of thinking about yourself that stands aloof from the successes and failures of daily life. It's about a sense of self-worth that has nothing to do with what people think or how you are doing. By choosing to stand apart from other people's judgments, this is an esteem that you award to yourself.

As our imaginary student seminar progresses, probing and questioning, the confusion intensifies. 'So what precisely is "worth"?' you ask. 'Is there a scale of "self-value" I can measure myself against? How do I know when I have enough? Perhaps self-"worth" is something I just declare to be the case, while pouring myself into the "existential moment" and "seizing the day"?' There are puzzled frowns around the room.

'But does it matter?' interrupts one of the students. 'Doesn't it come down to the "elephant test"? Something hard to describe, but you know one when you see it?'[2] Heads seem to be nodding. We may be using the word with different meanings, the students are beginning to argue, but aren't we all really talking about the same thing? And does it really matter? The group thinks that they are on to something.

Here you take issue with the students. You tell them that you think it matters a great deal, because definitions have power. Definitions shape the way we think. By imposing a perceptual 'filter' on the world, they adjudicate the things we 'see' and those we don't. So if the issue is important, then it's more important still that we define our terms. A student interjects, 'But this is the sort of thing that academic psychologists get paid to sort out, isn't it? So what do they say?' Again, heads are nodding in agreement. You respond by telling them the story of Nathaniel Branden.

In the heady days of the 1960s when the self-esteem movement really began to take off, a psychologist called Nathaniel Branden rose to prominence as one of its big-name thinkers. Once linked with the objectivist philosopher Ayn Rand, and a promoter of her thinking, Branden is one of the smartest and most articulate contributors to the self-esteem story of the last half-century (and certainly not a supporter of simplistic boosterism). In 1969 he published one of the early-landmark volumes on this theme, *The Six Pillars of Self-Esteem*.

In 1990 Branden stood before a major international conference on self-esteem and declared, 'We recognize that, just as a human being cannot hope to realize his or her potential without healthy self-esteem, neither can a society whose members do not value themselves . . . Self-esteem is an idea whose time has come.' This is heady stuff. The self-esteem idea can't be accused of lack of ambition. According to Branden, this isn't just about individual redemption; it's about the renaissance of whole societies. But he went on to say that, two decades after the publication of his book, there remained one outstanding issue: 'We must take responsibility . . . for clarifying for ourselves and others what precisely self-esteem means [as otherwise] we run the risk not only of failing to produce worthwhile results but also of discrediting the field.'[3] Good point. As we noted earlier, definitions matter. We may be surprised that Branden is still needing to make the point a full twenty-five years after the birth of the self-esteem movement, but at least the problem is being addressed.

Back in our student seminar, jaws drop around the room when you disclose that, two decades later in 2008, a full forty years after the publication of his landmark book, Branden blogged these words: 'If asked what I see as immediate challenges facing those who work in the field of self-esteem, either as researchers or as practitioners, I will answer . . . that the first priority is to carve out a definition of self-esteem that researchers can agree on. No easy task, in my opinion.'[4]

The students are staggered by this discovery. 'What? You mean millions of research dollars have been spent, thousands upon thousands of academic papers litter our libraries, the "compelling discoveries of modern psychology" have been rolled out in school-based self-esteem programmes across the US and Europe, countless self-help manuals and an endless stream of psychobabble spewed forth by an army of psychological gurus . . . and we still don't have an agreed definition?!'

'Branden isn't alone in his view,' you reassure them. 'One of the most cogent and incisive thinkers among the academic psychologists still researching this area recently lamented, " . . . It turns out that some researchers define self-esteem in one way, others define it different ways, and . . . although a lot of people may talk about self-esteem, little communication occurs."'[5] At this point our student seminar breaks up in confusion. Lopsided beginnings almost always result in skewed endings, and this is precisely where we have landed.

Lopsided beginnings almost always result in skewed endings, and this is precisely where we have landed.

The philosophic muddle

Everything ends in philosophy, and here we discover two more problems for self-esteem ideology. First, who or what is the real 'self' that we are trying to esteem? And secondly, why (and on what basis) should we value and esteem the self anyway? Would we encourage Hitler to esteem himself? Or Pol Pot? Both of these questions are deeply philosophical and raise complicated issues.

What is a self?

Where is the 'you', the inner self that needs to be so cherished and esteemed? Is it the same you that played 'pass the parcel' as a five-year-old? If so, in what sense? You don't look the same, you certainly don't feel the same and you are not made precisely of the same thing. Moreover, will it be the same you that will one day languish in a care home with your memory failing, so that you are no longer able to recall that game at all? In all sorts of ways, the 'you' that looks at life through the eyes of a five-year-old is quite different from the elderly 'you' struggling to remember what you saw. Who or what is the self that we attempt to esteem as we migrate through the different experiences and stages of life? And is there a 'self' to love and count as worthy in there at all?

The great philosopher David Hume wrote, 'For my part, when I enter most intimately into what I call myself, I always stumble on some particular perception or other, of heat or cold, light or shade, love or hatred, pain or pleasure, colour or sound etc. I never catch myself distinct from such perception.'[6] What he meant was that, when we go looking for the 'real' me, all that we find is one thought tumbling after another amid a kaleidoscope of feelings, tunes, urges and drives. And that's all. When you go looking for the real you, like a handful of sand, it just slips through your fingers.

Philosophers have struggled with this conundrum for centuries. Is it better to think of there being a 'pearl' at the centre of personality that is the real me, a kind of inner observer that keeps track of our lives? Or is David Hume's 'bundle theory' of the self – a fluctuating experience of intertwining thoughts, feelings and desires that wax and wane over time but somehow manage to create the illusion of a self – the right explanation?[7]

The answer depends on your point of view. We are not about to solve this question here, but when the injunction to 'love yourself' is handed down by self-help gurus, we need to ask which 'self' they are talking about. As I look in the mirror, what precisely is the bit that I need to practise cherishing and 'feeling good' about? Is it the self that shouted at my wife yesterday? Or the self that reached into my pocket to give the waitress an extra-large tip? You will be surprised by the poverty of intellectual engagement with this question among academic psychologists and counsellors. The Christian psychologist Paul Vitz pretty much summed it up when he described their work as 'a masterpiece of woolly thinking':

> Of course, many examples of 'selves' . . . are given, but the examples . . . do not clarify some of the basic difficulties. For example: are there not many and conflicting parts and layers of the self? Certainly such conflict between different self-goals, different ideals, and so forth, is a common experience. If so, which is the 'real' self? How does one choose among the various selves? If it is claimed there is only one 'true' self, or that different 'true' selves do not conflict, what is the basis for the claim?[8]

Quite.

Because I'm worthless?

I once came across a wall poster by the Bristol street artist Banksy that showed a bedraggled-looking rat squatting by a rough brick wall, with a paintbrush dripping in her hand. She had just daubed a piece of graffiti: 'Because I'm worthless'.

The term *self*-esteem rests on the notion that you can award value, worth and meaning to yourself. It supposes that you can say how much you are worth. But just how much is that? *Why* should you 'love' or 'esteem' yourself? What have you done to deserve it? In the absence of an objective assessment or declaration of worth that comes from beyond the self, what exactly is the basis for self-esteem? What scale of reference will you use?

Judgments about worth and value can't be derived within the categories of scientific thought. The famous behavioural psychologist B. F. Skinner pressed home this point by asking how a humanistic therapist (such as Carl Rogers) is supposed to respond if a client chooses to become a more accomplished liar. He questioned why we should simply believe that setting somebody free to value themselves and consider themselves 'special' will unleash a force for good in the human personality: 'Is the self-chosen goal independent of his [the client's] early ethical and religious training? Of the opinions and attitudes of others who are important to him? Surely not.'[9] But time and again in self-esteem ideology, this fundamental question simply gets glossed over.

Albert Ellis, one of the founding fathers of 'cognitive' approaches to therapy, has been the most courageous and clear-thinking critic in this area. In his classic work, *The Myth of Self-Esteem*, Ellis highlights the problem:

> If the individual's perception of his own value, or worth, so importantly affects his thoughts, emotions, and actions, how is it possible to help him consistently to appraise himself so that, no matter what kind of performances he achieves and no matter how popular or unpopular . . . he almost invariably accepts or respects himself? Oddly enough, modern psychotherapy has not often posed this question – at least not in the form just stated.[10]

Ellis is saying that it is illogical to suppose that we can respect and value ourselves, regardless of what the 'self' actually thinks and the good and evil that it gets up to.

Ellis is also sceptical about the blind faith fostered by humanist psychotherapists like Carl Rogers: 'Rogers . . . really seems to [think] that the individual can be accepted, can accept himself, without reference to . . . achievement; or that . . . he can accept himself just because he is he, because he is alive, because he exists.'[11] As their victims would attest, Hitler, Pol Pot and a multitude of other notorious perpetrators of evil have been only too 'alive' and 'existing'. What is the basis on which they should accept and value themselves? The self-theorists will probably respond that their evil deeds stemmed from their refusal or inability to do just that, to accept themselves. But that is the kind of circular argument that leads us down a philosophical cul-de-sac. The merits of raising people's self-esteem aren't true simply because we assert them to be so.

Modern existentialist philosophers have tried to tackle the thorny question of how an individual can continue to view herself as a person of value and worth, even when she is behaving in a discreditable and undeserving way. How should we understand our value or worth, asked Heidegger and Jean-Paul Sartre, when so much of our moment-by-moment experience seems to be shaped and determined by accidents of birth and random influences over which we have no control? Their answer is to focus on the subjectivity of experience: the 'I' that experiences the different options open to us and the 'I' that experiences itself as choosing freely between them. Moral goodness is defined as the extent to which I fulfil my own definition of myself. As one philosopher put it, 'The more . . . I am conscious of myself, the more, and the more clearly, I define myself – the more I am a good person.'[12]

Get that? No, I don't either. Existentialism is hard to grasp, but some of the more practical ideas have been adopted (and adapted) by various therapists attracted to its emphasis on the value of human choice. The client is invited to reflect on their experience in a way that insists that they, and they alone, can choose between the competing demands and expectations that filter through from their experience. Their value as human beings lies in the fact that the moment of choice belongs only to them.

This is a perfectly valid point of view, provided that you accept the tenets of existentialism. No matter how you may have wrecked your life or the lives of other people, if you 'choose' to be special, you can become special. Indeed, it carries over rather well into postmodernism. If you declare yourself to be 'special', well . . . who can argue with that? Everybody has a point of view, so good luck to you. So you can opt to be an existentialist if that suits you. Just don't try to dress it up as 'science' or 'psychology'.

The way we approach the question of how to think about ourselves depends profoundly on our worldview. In the next chapter I begin to argue for the coherence and grandeur of the Christian worldview as a basis of self-understanding. But first I want to round up this brief survey of the conceptual muddle surrounding self-esteem ideology by touching further on the work of three secular psychologists who have at least attempted to grapple with some of the wider philosophical problems.

Albert Ellis – Think rationally about yourself

Albert Ellis has a simple solution: he doesn't even bother with the concept of self-esteem. Ellis founded the school of 'Rational Emotive Therapy' which practises ruthless logic in the way that we think about ourselves. Ellis attacks self-esteem ideology as philosophically vacuous and conceptually absurd. You will never be able to award yourself a 'value' independently of what you think, do and achieve, he says, so you should give up trying and get on with your life. Equally, if you don't have a 'given' definition of what it means to be human that comes from a religious worldview, accept the logic of your position and stop trying to rate, grade or judge your 'worth' altogether:

> There is a . . . choice that is much more philosophically elegant, less definitional, and more likely to conform to empirical reality. That is the seldom posited assumption that value is a meaningless term when applied to a person's being, that it is invalid to call him either 'good' or 'bad', and that if educators and psychotherapists can teach people to . . . have no 'self'-images whatever, they may considerably help the human dilemma and enable men and women to be much less emotionally disturbed than they now tend to be.[13]

Ellis distinguishes carefully between rating (or scoring) *individual* attributes, gifts and behaviours, and grading ourselves more generally. We should continue to make judgments about *individual* attributes and behaviours ('I work hard at my job which is good, but neglect my wife which is bad'), but stop making evaluations about ourselves as whole people ('I am a good person' or 'I am a valuable, worthy person').

If you think about it, says Ellis, it's simply illogical to attempt to give some kind of score to yourself as a total human being. You are composed of hundreds and thousands of individual traits which result in a variety of actions, some that can be judged good and some bad. Even the same action may have been perfectly executed one day, but hopelessly failed the day afterwards. So instead of attempting to arrive at some overall global score for yourself, confine yourself to rating and judging individual behaviours and stop rating *yourself* altogether. Develop skills-confidence rather than *self*-confidence.

Ellis has an interesting approach that simply buries the hatchet on the big philosophical questions and tries to help the client in a 'just-do-it' sort of way. Rather than agonizing about yourself, trying to get your self-judgments and scores out of the doldrums with boosterism, stop rating yourself altogether. Instead, says Ellis, focus on developing your strengths and your confidence in specific areas: just because you are the fastest runner in the world or the greatest trombone player doesn't have anything to say about you as a person. It just says something about your trombone playing or your athleticism. You may be hopeless at keeping accurate accounts or holding an intelligent conversation for longer than a couple of minutes, but that doesn't make you a bad *person*. And so Ellis concludes,

> I do not have intrinsic worth or worthlessness, but merely aliveness. I'd better rate my traits and acts but not my totality or 'self'. I fully *accept* myself, in the sense that I know I have aliveness, and I *choose* to survive and live as happily as possible, and with minimum needless pain. I only require this knowledge and this choice – *and no other kind of self-rating.*[14]

Sounds reasonable? In the absence of a worldview that is capable of handling the big questions of our significance, it's certainly logical. And in the light of the concerns we have raised about the dangers of boosterism, his call to debunk such efforts and concentrate on individual strengths has much to commend it.

Martin Seligman – Be realistic about yourself

Martin Seligman, founder and leader of what has come to be called the 'Positive Psychology Movement', has developed his thinking along similar lines.[15] Seligman is deeply critical of the 'boosterism' of the self-esteem movement because it ignores the often cruel realities of human nature: 'Whilst boosterism was energising, it was footless, almost dishonest . . . '[16] He argues instead for the more rational 'in-between' [*sic*] of *healthy self-appraisal*. Like Ellis, Seligman encourages people away from making global self-judgments, and urges them instead to focus on individual thoughts and dispute illogical and harmful patterns.

Seligman rejects blind optimism, parroting phrases such as, 'Every day in every way, I am getting better.' It's about the realistic 'in-between' of tackling 'thinking biases', such as always interpreting events in 'catastrophic' terms or assuming that we or other people are 'always' to blame, and so on. Seligman's philosophic focus is towards the individual in context, learning to think realistically about life's adversities, rather than with the breezy optimism of 'boosterism'.

Many of Seligman's ideas have been taken up in resilience and 'bounce-back' programmes in the UK and the US. A number of organizations work on this 'positive-psychology' agenda, cultivating resilience, perseverance, courage and confidence, without getting bogged down in self-esteem ideology. Christians who are concerned about the philosophical and practical dangers of self-esteem should broadly welcome the emerging emphasis on resilience. These programmes are essentially practical, focused on building good relationships and developing self-awareness. They duck the deeper philosophical problems, but their emphasis on realistic assessments of ourselves and getting involved with the needs of others at least fits into a Christian worldview, rather than cutting across its key assumptions.

Jennifer Crocker – Look beyond yourself

Another interesting contributor to this field is the American psychologist Jennifer Crocker. Crocker has published a series of studies that prove the dangerous and toxic effects of setting goals for ourselves based on how good they make us feel. Inevitably, she says, the desire to feel good gets hijacked by other people's judgments of our worth and value, and we become enslaved to *looking good*.[17]

In one of her experiments Crocker investigated students whose self-worth and sense of significance were heavily dependent on 'staying up there' in terms of academic ability.[18] These were people who staked their pursuit of *feeling good* on *looking good* academically. She found that students like this were much less interested in learning for its own sake. Their real goal was to 'feel good' about themselves by defending a self-image constructed around academic prowess. For them, learning was simply a tool, a way of outperforming others and validating that self-image. What mattered was *how I look*, not *what I learn*.

In order to explore how this mindset affected their capacity to care about other people, she played the sort of dirty trick that psychologists often spring upon their unsuspecting volunteers. She gave all her subjects an intellectual exercise to complete, after which half were told (regardless of their actual performance) that they'd failed pretty badly, and the other half were told nothing at all. The students were then given what they thought was an unrelated exercise which involved listening to a 'personal problem' being poured out by one of her accomplices. The person who had confided her unhappy situation then 'rated' the target subjects on how well they had listened, how compassionate they had appeared and how much she had liked them. Who do you think were the better listeners?

You are right, the students with the greatest need to look good academically showed the least empathy and were the most disliked. While the victims poured out their traumatic stories, these students appeared bored and preoccupied, and were the most prone to interrupting. They were just too gutted about having fallen below their desired self-image to worry about the needs of others. And so, argues Crocker, 'Pursuing self-esteem interferes with establishing and maintaining mutually supportive relationships, because people become focused on themselves at the expense of others' needs and feelings.' In other studies too Crocker illustrates how the pursuit of self-esteem undermines and interferes with our capacity for self-control, learning and being independently minded.

But hold on! At this point counsellors will be queuing up to remind me that the whole point about 'self-acceptance' is that we should learn to value ourselves, *regardless of our successes or failures*. They will say that Crocker's work identifies the very problem for which the self-esteem movement provides the solution. No, they will say, of course we shouldn't stake our sense of self-esteem on our abilities or what other people think or say. Instead we should aim for what psychologists call 'non-contingent' self-esteem – self-worth that isn't dependent on anything or anybody else. The only thing that should matter to us is what we think about ourselves. So we need to be ourselves, love ourselves, and hence the core project is to *esteem* ourselves.

But, as Jennifer Crocker points out, although in theory the pursuit of 'non-contingent' self-esteem sounds logical, 'it is not clear whether people with truly non-contingent self-worth actually exist . . . Research has identified very few people who appear to have non-contingent self-esteem.'[19] This is a staggering claim. What does she mean? Crocker is saying that we are so in the grip of insecurity and anxiety about status, so trained by our culture to think in terms of 'winners and losers' that trying to 'just love yourself', regardless of what you achieve, and, more crucially, regardless of what others notice that you achieve, is just about impossible. And so we end up 'running on a treadmill – despite enormous effort you never really get there'.[20]

Crocker's solution is to move away from the focus on ourselves to what she calls 'eco-awareness'. She teaches that we need to widen the lens and pull back our perspective, so that we are no longer focused solely on ourselves, but on the bigger eco-picture of which we are just one part. And then we can aim for what is good for others as well as what is good for ourselves. We need a 'part-of-something-bigger-than-me' mindset, she argues.

As with Seligman's ideas, there is much in Crocker's work for Christians to welcome, and, as we shall see later, she has carried out considerable research that demonstrates the psychological benefits of adopting a 'part-of-something-bigger-than-me' mindset. But the core philosophical problem remains unanswered: it sounds good – but why should I? If I choose to aim for the common good, what happens when I miss? How do I deal with guilt and shame? We may want to belong to something bigger than ourselves, but what happens when we don't know what that is?

A worldview issue

There is something about the human spirit that longs for meaning and significance: 'Our hearts are restless until they find their rest in Thee [God].'[21] The subjective experience of insecurity and homelessness spoken of here by Augustine is deeply rooted in the spiritual dimension of life. On the one hand, there's an instinctive awareness of nobility, perhaps even grandeur, about our humanity, but, on the other hand, we sense an equally deep-rooted alienation and dislocation gnawing at the centre of self-awareness. Cultivating 'eco-awareness' as a response to selfism, as Jennifer Crocker suggests, barely seems to scratch the surface of this dilemma.

Self-esteem ideology raises profound questions about the nature and destiny of humankind that can't be answered satisfactorily within the reductionist categories of experimental psychology. We cannot *signify ourselves*. We need a comprehensive and philosophically coherent worldview, capable of addressing the big questions of significance in terms of who we are and how we came to be.

The journey that took us nowhere

And so we have arrived at the end of psychology's big ego trip to discover that, without a coherent worldview, our journey has hit the buffers. It's a dead end. We have investigated the orthodoxies of the self-esteem movement, weighed them in the balance and found them to be wanting. On almost any measure you care to mention – precision of terminology, evidence of beneficial effect, potential for harm, philosophical integrity – self-esteem ideology promised big but delivered small. It's time to turn back and set out on a different path. We need to discover how to unravel the effects of this cultural epidemic of self-veneration on our hearts and lives. And then we must find a more satisfactory way to address the issues that drove us into the arms of self-esteem ideology in the first place.

But where can we find a worldview, an over-arching perspective, capable of embracing these challenges? I believe the Christian worldview provides the coherent narrative that we long for. The Christian faith rests on the central proposition that God has revealed himself in the Bible, and pivotally in the person and work of Jesus Christ – the 'Word' of God made flesh. This revelation cracks open a reality in which, on the one hand, human beings are found standing at the pinnacle of creation's glory, rendered in the image of God himself and therefore of immense worth and value. On the other hand, it confronts us with the spectre of 'fallen' humankind under the judgment of a fiercely just and righteous God, and therefore riven with guilt, shame and insecurity.

The Christian revelation in the Bible speaks of a divine verdict: people 'fall short' of God's glory; there is division into sheep and goats; and a separation into those on the right hand and those on the left. It confronts us with death as the consequence ('wages') of our rebellion and with separation from our Creator. In moments of ruthless honesty and self-awareness, we sense these realities. The price we pay is a latent sense of insecurity, peppered with moments of outright terror. We attempt to plug our aching insecurity with 'self-esteem', but in our hearts we know that it simply will not do. There is something broken at the core of human experience and we need something better, deeper and more coherent to satisfy our spiritual yearning.

For the remainder of this book I am going to explore the biblical worldview that I believe addresses these ultimate questions, as well as providing a framework for the management of our rebel emotions and our experiences of self. The Bible does not claim to offer an exhaustive account of human psychological experience. It isn't a substitute for a textbook of psychology or sociology. Instead it claims that all truth is God's truth, and then it sets the parameters by which we can interpret and 'story' our observations about human experience, including the discoveries of experimental psychology.

And so, in the brief space allowed, I will attempt to integrate some of the insights gained from psychological thought within the framework of biblical teaching about the nature and destiny of humankind.

Later, when we come to deal with some of the very practical and personal implications of this, I will need to assume that the reader is committed to a Christian worldview anchored in the Bible, while in no way intending to exclude those who are not so persuaded. But whatever our view, there's no quick-fix here. Psychology couldn't provide us with a one-stop solution to the turmoil of emotions we feel about ourselves, and neither, if we're honest, does the Christian gospel. We are not going to make the mistake, as do so many Christian books on self-esteem, of simply concocting a Christian version of boosterism.

Whether it's feelings of insecurity, longing for significance, problems with confidence or unremitting self-hatred, these are different domains of experience that need specific responses, integrating relevant psychological insights within the broad framework of Christian revelation. And so, as we turn to examine the Christian view of humankind, we begin with the great creation narratives found in the earliest books of the Bible: What is a human being? How did we come into being? And, most crucially, what are we made *for*?

9. WE DID IT MY WAY

Most of our life is in large part a rationalization
of our failure to find out who we really are,
what our basic strength is, what thing it is that
we were meant to work upon the world.
Ernst Becker[1]

I've just arrived back from Rome, one of my favourite holiday destinations. If you've ever wandered around her architectural sights, like me you will have noticed how difficult it is to figure out what it all once looked like. So I get quite inspired by those clever little pocket books that allow you to lay a transparency of the original structure over the top of a picture of what remains. Now, at a stroke, the scene before me springs into life. This heap of old rubble, I realize, is in fact a glorious ruin.

Human beings are truly awesome. Reflect on the boldness and ingenuity of human artistic endeavour, our intellectual stature, our feats of sporting prowess, our gifts of organizational engineering. Human resilience and bounce-back, sometimes in the face of unrivalled odds and adversity, inspire wonder and admiration. And yet, on the other hand, these same creatures are capable of staggering acts of cruelty, mindless destructiveness and mind-boggling deceit.

Like ancient Rome herself, humans are a busted flush, a glorious ruin.

The metaphor of the glorious ruin, attributed to the great Christian teacher and apologist Francis Schaeffer, captures the essence of the human dilemma. But while even a cursory glance at creation and human history confirms its gruesome reality, it is only when we look at ourselves through the pages of the Bible (a bit like holding one of those transparencies over a picture of the rubble before you) that we can see the full scale of the disaster.

You can rule the world

The Bible tells us that we were created to reflect the nature of God himself. In fact, we don't simply 'reflect' his nature. The Bible goes much further. We have been created *in the image and likeness of God* (Genesis 1:26–27). But what does this mean?

Being made in the image of God means that we bear his likeness, both in what we are and in what we do. The spiritual awareness that separates us from animals, the qualities that allow us to dream, invent, govern, choose and direct, reflect something deep and profound about the nature of God. In other words, human consciousness is designed so that it 'works' in a way that echoes something of the way that God 'works'. It means that humans are not only superior to all other created beings in a quantitative sense (cleverer, more intuitive, etc.), but in a qualitative (different league) sense too. Thus, God places great value on us: it's wrong to take the life of a human, because, even after the fall, we are still patterned after the image of God (Genesis 9:6).

Humans are called to be 'image-doers' as well as image-bearers. In Genesis 1:26–27 Adam and Eve's being made in the likeness of God was qualified in terms of their mandate to exert dominion over the world. They were called to rule as God rules. Dominion wasn't simply about maintenance either; it was about creative direction and growth. Adam and Eve's joint lordship over the world was intended to translate into real authority and real governing responsibility. Moreover, as they expressed and fulfilled God's image in the concrete adventures of governance, the first humans stood to gain an even deeper, richer relationship with God. So right from the beginning, the human condition (although perfect) wasn't intended to be a static thing. It was experienced as something with potential for growth and development.[2] As one author puts it, 'Human identity was not finished at creation, but was to be perfected [even further] by fulfilling the trial of the original covenant, winning the right to eat from the tree of everlasting life and blessedness.'[3]

Gloriously ruined

But humans didn't fulfil the trial of the original covenant (or 'agreement') which set out the terms and conditions of human rule. In an act of rebellion they became derailed from their divine mission and, as a result, spiralled downwards into greed and destructiveness. Here is how the secular British philosopher John Gray characterizes the human condition as we find it now: 'Humans use what they know to meet their most urgent needs – even if the result is ruin . . . When times are desperate they act to protect their offspring, to revenge their enemies, or simply to give vent to their feelings. *These are not flaws that can be remedied*' [emphasis mine].[4]

Gray argues that science (including modern psychology) can't rescue us, because 'the uses of knowledge will always be as shifting and crooked as humans are themselves'.[5] In Gray's opinion, this spells the eventual destruction of the species and indeed the end of the world. For 'what could be more hopeless than placing the Earth in the charge of this exceptionally destructive species? It is not of becoming the planet's wise stewards that Earth-lovers dream, but of a time when humans have ceased to matter.'[6]

Gray's analysis, based on observation, is close to what Scripture teaches as a matter of first principle. Human destiny has been derailed, and subsequently forfeited, in an act of deliberate rebellion. The resulting dislocation has introduced profound disorder into the human psyche, and this, in turn, has spawned a raft of social, psychological and ecological problems. The Bible calls this 'twist', or dislocation, in the structure of human personality: 'sin'.

We can (still) rule the world!

It's really all about pride. Focusing on individual sins misses the unique biblical message that sin is essentially a cognitive schema, a 'way of looking at the world' that is prideful or 'full' with pride. Scratch the surface of individual sins and you will find beneath an aspiration to be like God (Genesis 3:5), a rejection of dependence and a refusal to take God at his word. The apostle Paul puts it like this:

> Although they knew God, they neither glorified him as God nor gave thanks to him, but their thinking became futile and their foolish hearts were darkened. Although they claimed to be wise, they became fools and exchanged the glory of the immortal God for images made to look like mortal man and birds and animals and reptiles.
>
> (Romans 1:21–23)

Paul takes this analysis one step further when he says that, in the last days, 'people will be lovers of themselves' (2 Timothy 3:2). In Paul's teaching, the ultimate idolatry, the very root of sin, is self-worship.

The many faces of self-admiration

We see human pride played out at many levels, but perhaps no more tellingly than in what psychologists call the 'cognitive biases' of human personality. For example, take 'confirmation bias'. This is a tendency only to 'see' those things which confirm what we already know.[7] Market researchers have shown how car owners often prefer to read advertisements about their own marque, while largely ignoring those for others. We tend to associate with people who are like us too. And studies among athletes show how, in order to preserve 'self-esteem', they often credit themselves for success, but blame external factors, such as bad refereeing, for failure.

'Better than average' is another form of self-serving bias. In one well-known study, groups of individuals were given a task and then asked to rate their performance in relation to the performance of the rest of the group. All of the subjects evaluated themselves as being above average, compared to the rest of the group. In fact, the lowest-scoring group (those in the bottom quartile) showed the largest 'better-than-average' bias of all, suggesting that those with the least skill also had the greatest difficulty in recognizing it.[8]

Then there's 'hindsight bias', or, better, the 'knew-that' phenomenon. We are all aware of people who, when a new fact emerges or a situation gets clarified, somehow 'knew that' all along. Their conversation is peppered with phrases such as 'of course' and 'quite'. In one study,[9] psychologists gave one half of a group of students a made-up finding such as, 'Social psychologists have found that, whether choosing friends or falling in love, we are most attracted to people whose traits are different from our own. There seems to be wisdom in the old saying "opposites attract".' The other half were then shown a statement that summarized the exact opposite 'finding': 'Social psychologists have found that, whether choosing friends or falling in love, we are most attracted to people whose traits are similar to our own. There seems to be wisdom in the old saying that "birds of a feather flock together".' When they instructed their subjects to judge whether they found these results 'surprising' or 'not surprising', a majority in both groups said 'not surprising', or, 'I could have told you that'. There is nothing more reassuring than being wise after the event.

Sin blinds us to these biases in our personality. In Mark's Gospel we read how James and John, two of Jesus' most trusted followers (both were selected to witness his transfiguration), respond to Jesus' dramatic announcement of his savage and humiliating death with an embarrassing level of self-absorption: 'Teacher . . . we want you to do for us whatever we ask . . . Let one of us sit at your right and the other at your left in your glory' (Mark 10:35–37). Whatever was going on here? Couldn't these men 'see' their naked ambition? As the psalmist reminds us,

> In his own eyes he flatters himself
>> too much to detect or hate his sin.
> (Psalm 36:2)

The consequences of sin

As we can see, the consequences of the fall were profound and far-reaching. Our revolt against heaven ricocheted through creation and dislocated our relationship with the world, with one another and with ourselves. Most importantly, it severed our relationship with God and brought us under his judgment. This has been accompanied by a profound insecurity in our sense of belonging: to the world, to one another and even within our own psyche. As a result, our hearts are restless and, like Cain, we wander the face of the earth with nowhere to 'be' (Genesis 4:12). But what does this insecurity look and feel like? How does it play out in our everyday lives?

The metaphysical dimension of insecurity

In his Pulitzer Prize-winning work, *The Denial of Death*, the cultural anthropologist Ernest Becker writes, 'Man is literally split in two: he has an awareness of his own splendid uniqueness in that he sticks out of nature with a towering majesty, and yet he goes back into the ground a few feet in order to blindly and dumbly rot and disappear forever. It is a terrifying dilemma to be in and to have to live with.'[10]

Becker is saying that we sense something of our glory, yet can't figure out how it 'fits' with our flawed and destructive nature, and particularly the terrifying fact of our own mortality. So, argues Becker, all human behaviour is pursued ultimately to defend ourselves against the chilling inevitability of death. Behind the centuries-old rituals of the world's great religions lurks one simple reality: a desperate need for belief – any belief will do – provided that it is capable of eclipsing the dread reality of our own destruction and shoring up our self-belief.

Interestingly, Becker's work has inspired the development of a new school of psychology that views our efforts at self-esteem as a form of 'terror management'.[11] Its originators suggest that, as religious belief crumbled in the face of scientific advances, we needed another defence against death, a different kind of belief: '[Self-esteem is] a protective shield designed to control the potential terror that results from awareness of the horrifying possibility that we humans are merely transient animals groping to survive in a meaningless universe.'[12]

Do you see what these psychologists are saying? They are telling us that, in a post-religious world, the reassurance that humans once sought in their great cathedrals and temple rituals are now being found in paradigms of self-worth that we have constructed in our own psyches. Hovering precariously above haunting insecurity and psychological terror, our fragile self-esteem is simply our latest line of defence against the realities of our own extinction.

If we buy into this theory, and I think there is something in it, it speaks of a metaphysical ambivalence deep in the human heart: pride intertwined with insecurity. This is why our attempts at 'non-contingent' self-esteem never really work. Despite our best efforts to love and value ourselves, regardless of what we achieve or how we look, it's never quite good enough. And so we are driven back to image-management, trying to draw from others the recognition and approval that we can't convincingly drum up for ourselves.

The moral dimension of insecurity

There is another kind of latent insecurity in the human heart that stems from guilt and shame. As we saw earlier in this chapter, in the eyes of God, human beings have true moral culpability. We stand condemned and under judgment. This results both in feelings of guilt and the experience of shame. But what's the difference?

The Bible tells us that we live in a moral universe, and that, being created in the image of God, humans have a sense of his law embedded in their hearts. In fact, it says that God's law is 'written on our hearts' and that our conscience 'bears witness' to it (Romans 2:15). When we break this law in individual acts of wrongdoing, we experience the unpleasant emotion of guilt. And guilt breeds insecurity, manifest in the unpleasant feeling of a 'guilty conscience'. Shame, another reflection of a guilty conscience, is something different, however. As guilt is the emotion linked to specific wrongs that I commit, shame is the emotion that stems from *being the kind of person that does that sort of thing*. Shame, indeed, is the emotion of inferiority.[13]

Let me give you an example of shame. I remember, as a very young boy, being involved in receiving stolen goods. The goods took the form of a single peanut, offered by a friend who, in a moment of severe moral lapse while the grocer's back was turned, had quietly removed a couple of them from the shop counter. To my shame, like Adam, I looked at the prohibited fruit, and I took and I ate. A deeply unpleasant wave of emotion swept through me like a storm, and, on arriving home, I blurted out the whole sorry tale. I was hardly prepared for what happened next. My father, disappointed, incensed and mortified, immediately marched me back to the grocer's to make a full confession. Momentarily, my pride stirred in protest. It was only ONE peanut, for goodness sake! But it wasn't simply that I'd accepted a stolen peanut. What really got to my father was that *his son was capable of doing such a thing*, that it should ever have crossed my mind to behave in such a way. Visibly shrinking in his eyes, I longed for the ground to open up and for somewhere to hide. As I tell you this story, I can feel it again: shame – the emotion of inferiority.

The psycho-social dimension of insecurity
But shame isn't always linked to moral culpability and guilt. There were many other moments of shame in my childhood

(as there probably were in yours) that had nothing to do with wrongdoing. On these occasions the explanation was more psychological and social than moral. For example, I was never a particularly good trumpet player. In fact, if I remember correctly, when I auditioned for a local youth orchestra, they assigned me to the role of 'third trumpet'. In truth, I shouldn't have been offered a place at all, but I could be quite charming and, as the youngest member, I think they quite liked the idea of having a mascot. It didn't take me long to disabuse them of that fantasy.

On one fateful evening during a 'very important' public performance I was quietly counting my rest bars when my mind wandered off . . . Suddenly, in a moment of high musical drama, the whole orchestra stopped playing and the conductor pointed his baton directly at me. Yes, me! There was no doubt about it. There it was again. Me! I couldn't remember having a solo part, but, in a moment of panic, I lifted my trumpet to my lips and played the next note on the music sheet. My dissonant blast sounded for a second or two, before being overwhelmed by the sound of deep, rolling thunder coming from behind me. Oh no – of course, everybody had been waiting for the drum roll that heralded the finale! The conductor had been pointing to the percussion section *behind* me, not *at* me! I was flooded with feelings of shame. Hot and sweaty, a dreadful red blotching began to spread up from my chest, over my neck and then slowly over my face. Believing that every eye in the entire auditorium was glaring disapprovingly in my direction, I prayed for the ground to open up, so that I could shrink out of existence. Shame – the emotion of inferiority.

What was going on here? I hadn't committed a sin; I'd made a mistake. I'd failed to live up to expectations and, by punctur-ing an otherwise splendid performance with my musical

mishap, had brought the whole orchestra into public dis-
approval, or so it seemed. I had fallen short of the impression
that I wanted to present to the world, and indeed the picture
I wanted to present to myself. And I felt ashamed.

These kinds of experiences are about *living* in a fallen world,
rather than *sinning* in a fallen world. You will remember that,
as part of the judgment meted out after the fall, Adam was
told that the ground would be cursed and that 'through painful
toil you will eat of it all the days of your life. It will produce
thorns and thistles for you . . . ' (Genesis 3:18). Life in a fallen
world is hard. It is slow to yield its metaphorical fruits, and we
gather them in the face of hardship, setbacks and frequent
disappointments. Also, just as Adam blamed Eve, and Eve
blamed the serpent, in the aftermath of the fall we inhabit an
atmosphere of blame, suspicion and rivalry. And when we fail,
in our own eyes or the eyes of other people, we experience the
deeply uncomfortable emotion of inferiority: shame.

Of course, as the psychoanalysts remind us, shame reactions
can be cultivated by the way in which we have been treated in
early childhood, as well as by our failures and mistakes in the
here and now. For example, pushy parents with high expectations, or hyper-critical parents who demand perfection, may
help shape strong attachments to 'image' in their developing
child. Thus, when she fails to live up to expectations, she hits
the ground that much harder than other children. Human
competitiveness and judgmentalism also make it harder to fail,
amplifying our sense of exclusion and inferiority.

Experience of sexual or physical abuse can play a particularly powerful role in the genesis of shame and inferiority. I
think of Peter (name and details changed), a young married
man who, as a youngster, had been sexually abused by a
relative. On the surface he appeared a well-adjusted, confident
and godly man. Given his exceptional gifts, he had been

approached to take up the role of elder in his local Presbyterian church. To his surprise, this triggered an almost panic-stricken rerun of feelings that had lain buried for years. Peter was flooded with an emotion in which he felt almost physically diminished. He simply couldn't take on such a responsible, respectable role, with such shame in his history. As we talked through his early experiences (he had received some excellent pastoral and professional counselling a few years before), the pitiless nature of his systematic abuse by a trusted relative was all too painfully apparent. Clearly, Peter's experience of shame was more about sin done to him than about his own sin.

Reconciling shame and pride

How do we square such experiences with the biblical analysis of pride? To readers trained in secular models of psychotherapy and dealing with abused clients like Peter, the scriptural analysis of sin and pride can seem especially counter-intuitive. You have spent your professional careers listening to harrowing stories of abuse and parental neglect like his. You have heard heart-breaking narratives of astonishing mental cruelty, designed to crush a child's spirit and undermine her confidence. How can we expect people to develop confidence, and even a realistic view of themselves, when their self-attitudes have been mutilated in the crucible of so much abuse and neglect?

These are people who think themselves down, not those who push themselves up. They are the doormats, the first to volunteer when the washing-up needs doing and the last to ask for seconds. They are not people seeking recognition, but individuals who, perhaps for the first time in their lives, need to hear that they are accepted, that they have a place to be, that they are *worth something*. The anguished and pitiable stories that sometimes have to be coaxed out of damaged individuals in the therapist's counselling room present a compelling case against a biblical anthropology that identifies prideful sin at the root of human personality.

But if we stand back, there are several points of reconciliation. Pride characterizes our resistance to the word and the rule of God, rather than being a direct cause of every kind of unpleasant human psychological experience. We can't be held responsible for the sin done to us, and a loving, just and compassionate God would never hold us responsible. So it's crucially important to distinguish our sin from the sin done to us. In these situations, people need the time and space to talk through their experiences, feel their anger and rebuild a realistic sense of self.

Even in these situations, however, pride can soon make an appearance in the way that we deal with, or respond to, the sin done to us. There may be a refusal, for example, to become who God calls us to be and what he designed us to be. This doesn't diminish the culpability of those who may have inflicted harm on our psychological development, but it does insist that there is a place of responsibility for the way in which we respond to the sin done to us. Sometimes we come across people who persist in abusive situations, despite the terrible suffering involved, and a prideful or idealized view of themselves may linger behind that too. Similarly, those who constantly run down their contributions as second- and third-rate may need to be challenged about idolatries of perfection.[14] Although pride isn't a direct cause of all human psychological suffering, it isn't hard to find it lurking even in the most damaged human heart.

Leaving behind the myth of self-esteem

Drawing together these biblical insights, we can begin to understand why Christians have struggled for so long with the cult of self-esteem. As we've seen, even judged on its own terms within *psychological* categories of thought, the boosterism paradigm is naively simplistic and potentially harmful. But if we expose it to the *spiritual* dimensions of Christian faith, it is hopelessly inadequate. As I observed earlier, the temptation at this point would be to produce a Christian version of boosterism ('To God you're big stuff!') that buys into its basic assumptions and repeats its simplistic errors. However, instead we need to look carefully at the gap we are trying to plug with a boost to self-esteem and apply appropriate biblical, pastoral medicine to each specific situation. So let's take each of the three dimensions of insecurity – metaphysical, moral and psychosocial – and briefly explore the appropriate pastoral response. I should add that, in a book of this size, we can do little more than introduce the themes.

The metaphysical dimension of insecurity

The psychological school of 'terror-management' theory, inspired by the work of Ernst Becker (p. 139) teaches that self-esteem is a psychological defence against existential terror. To stave off the realities of our own unimportance and eventual extinction, we go to vast lengths to shore up the illusion of self-importance. Further, as we've seen, our capacity for self-deception has a powerful ally in the self-serving biases that operate in the human mind: confirmation bias and 'knew-that' bias. But as far as the Christian gospel is concerned, moments of spiritual restlessness, questioning, even downright terror, are a *blessing*, not a curse. They are servants of what the author Christopher Ash calls an 'awakened conscience',[15] a growing awareness that we are adrift from our Maker, that something has gone badly wrong with the world, and indeed that there is disorder in our own hearts. The simplistic blandishments of boosterism can be an ally in the hardening of conscience, promoting resistance to the gospel, because they shore up the illusion of self-importance. So there *is* no self-esteem solution to metaphysical insecurity. There is a gospel solution. As we shall see more fully in the next chapter, God in his grace has pursued us, paid the penalty for our sin at the cross and given us a new identity as loved sons or daughters. This is the only basis for a realistic view of ourselves that is grounded in truth, capable of dealing with ultimate questions of human existence.

The moral dimension of insecurity

The unpleasant emotions of guilt and shame may also be important messengers or servants of an awakened conscience. In our culture of self-admiration and entitlement, it's increasingly difficult to preach about sin and judgment, because it seems so hopelessly out of kilter with the cultural zeitgeist. Who wants to sell a message that hurts our pride? Who among us wants to learn that, understood in terms of sin and rebellion against God, we are not so 'special' after all? That's why so many churches are 'front-ending' the gospel with positive psychology messages, or re-engineering the pitch along the lines of human 'flourishing'.

The gospel *is* about flourishing, of course, but it is also about repentance, self-denial and the way of the cross. And we shouldn't duck that painful reality any more than a decent doctor would try to help her patient by ignoring the symptoms of a deadly disease. Experiences of guilt and

> *The gospel is about flourishing, of course, but it's also about repentance, self-denial and the way of the cross.*

shame are sometimes marks of what Paul, in his second letter to the church in Corinth, calls 'godly sorrow' that 'led you to repentance' (2 Corinthians 7:7–10). Note that Paul says that this kind of sorrow is 'as God intended' (verse 9). Why? Because it is temporary ('only for a little while') grit in the eye that has been put there for a purpose: to 'bring repentance' and to lead us to a place of forgiveness and cleansing. All too often in our self-esteem culture the importance of godly sorrow gets airbrushed out by positive messages of inclusion, acceptance and self-discovery.

Many years ago I was talking with a Christian who had been excluded from a leadership role in his church fellowship because of inappropriate sexual behaviour. Interestingly, his vicar had sent him for counselling. There were certainly events in his past that he needed to talk about and come to terms with, and, as we talked, it was clear that he had made signifi-cant strides forwards in self-awareness. But as this man continued talking about his early childhood and the insights he had gained, I became increasingly uneasy. Eventually I asked, 'John, those are really encouraging developments, and you've clearly made good progress in understanding yourself and dealing with some of the issues. But if I could just take you back to the event that led to your having to step aside from leadership in the church . . . What about confession and repentance? How has that been?'

John made some reassuring remarks, but clearly his energy and passion had been hijacked by the seductions of self-discovery and self-acceptance, not by the disciplines of confession and repentance. I left that conversation not at all sure that John had yet genuinely engaged with the reality of his sin, the damage he had done and the consequences he needed to face. How odd, I thought, that his vicar worries about counselling, and a psychiatrist is left asking questions about repentance. We mustn't allow the blandishments of self-esteem ideology to steal the deeper joy and contentment that flow from sin acknowledged and confessed and a conscience cleansed.

The psychosocial dimensions of insecurity

But not all guilt and shame has a direct relationship with personal sin. Exactly the same emotions can be generated by a range of adversities, early-life experience and mental health problems, as we saw earlier. I can only touch on these issues, but take depressive illness as one important example. For some people, feeling sad becomes more than a temporary reaction to life's disappointments and hardships, and it seems to take on a life of its own. Indeed, they become 'ill' with their sadness, finding themselves gripped by powerful emotions and twisted thoughts that seem to be generated from deep within their minds for no good cause. Besides biological features such as loss of appetite and weight, a classic symptom is to feel deeply hopeless about oneself, unworthy, irredeemably evil, and even suicidal. It is crucial in these circumstances that we receive the right kind of pastoral help, including, where needed, referral for professional care and the use of appropriate medication.

Even where there isn't a clinical depressive illness present, many people struggle with chronic negativity about their abilities or 'value' in the eyes of other people. Take the case of Timothy in the New Testament. In his letter to Timothy, Paul counsels him, 'God did not give us a spirit of timidity . . . ' (2 Timothy 1:7). In theologian John Stott's words, 'Humanly speaking, Timothy was hopelessly unfit to assume . . . weighty responsibilities of leadership in the church.'[16] It is clear from the contexts of Paul's counsel that he believes that Timothy is prone to 'fear' other people, and stands in need of encouragement and strengthening in his ministry. Timothy is still comparatively young: 'Don't let anyone look down on you because you are young . . . ' (1 Timothy 4:12) urges Paul. Also, he is prone to illness, with 'frequent illnesses' (1 Timothy 5:23). And it appears that he is uncomfortable and somewhat awkward in social situations, needing encouragement. So, for example, Paul feels he has to smooth his arrival in Corinth: 'If Timothy comes, see to it that he has nothing to fear while he is with you', and 'No one, then, should refuse to accept him (1 Corinthians 16:10, 11). It is likely too that Timothy depends on Paul and leans on his fatherly encouragement: Paul writes how he could not forget Timothy's tears when they had to go their separate ways (2 Timothy 1:4). So like Moses and Jeremiah before him, it seems that, when Timothy is thrust into the loathsome glare of the limelight, he finds himself in an acutely discomforting and disturbing place.

What was wrong with Timothy? We simply don't know. Timothy was the child of a mixed marriage, his father being Greek and his mother Jewish (Acts 16:1). In speaking of his spiritual development as a child, Paul only mentions his mother and grandmother (2 Timothy 1:5), but we have no idea about the various influences on the formation of Timothy's temperament, and it is pointless to indulge ourselves. Any number of early childhood influences, or the influences of inherited temperament, may have disposed Timothy to doubt his abilities and to feel judged and outclassed by other people. Whatever the cause, we are left with questions about how to deal with long-term feelings of insecurity about ourselves that are not directly related to sinful behaviour or a guilty conscience (or problems such as depression). How do we tackle tendencies, for whatever reason in our background, to harbour feelings of being judged or 'not good enough', or problems with confidence? Or those everyday experiences when we find ourselves looking for extra approval, trying to win people's attention or feeling judged for no good cause? These are the questions which we will shortly explore. But first, having discerned the importance of being realistic about sin, we will now explore the gift of being amazed by grace.

10. AMAZED BY GRACE

And I saw a mighty angel proclaiming in a loud voice,
'Who is worthy to break the seals and open the scroll?' . . .
I wept and wept because no-one was found
who was worthy to open the scroll
or look inside.
Revelation 5:2–4

Who is worthy? Good question. Are you worthy of a round of applause when you complete the marathon after months of hard work? You bet. But are you worthy of 'happiness'? The US National Association for Self-Esteem (NASE) thinks so. Its preferred definition of self-esteem is: 'the experience of being capable of meeting life's challenges and being *worthy* of happiness'.[1] In the world of self-esteem everybody deserves to feel good and is worthy of happiness .

But the biblical doctrine of sin hardly leads to the conclusion that we are worthy of happiness, or much else for that matter. So in this chapter we turn to consider two important questions. First, in terms of the gospel, in what sense can we be considered worthy? And secondly, does the Bible encourage us to pursue self-worth (in boosterism's sense of 'feeling good about myself') at all?

He loves us because we are worthy?

As I've indicated previously, this is the point at which so much Christian thought about self-esteem falls apart. Taking their cue from the self-esteem movement, Christian pastors and counsellors offer advice along the lines of: 'God would never have sent his only Son, his only precious Son, to die for junk – you're special!', and 'The very fact that Jesus died on a cross for you demonstrates how much you are worth.' Or as one counsellor puts it, 'Sinful men [and women] are valuable to God. If God loves sinful men for the redeemable value He sees in them, then we ought to love these men too, including ourselves.'[2] But is this a biblical approach to self-worth? I don't think so.

In the biblical concept of grace, the essence of God's movement towards us is that it happens despite, and not because of, what we are. The grounds for his saving work are lodged firmly, decisively, in the mystery of his sovereign will and purpose. Back in the Old Testament, for example, the Israelites were pretty firmly disabused of any lingering notions that they were called out of slavery because of their 'residual value' to God. In Deuteronomy God says to them, 'The LORD your God has chosen you out of all the peoples on the face of the earth to be his people, his treasured possession' (Deuteronomy 7:6). But what makes them so treasured? 'The LORD did not set his affection on you and choose you because you were more numerous than other peoples, for you were the fewest of all peoples. But it was because the LORD loved you and kept the oath he swore to your forefathers that he brought you out with a mighty hand and redeemed you . . . ' (Deuteronomy 7:7–8). The reason that God loves his people is, well, that he loves them.

What this means is that the *cause* of God's saving work isn't found in its recipients. It is hidden (with so many other answers to questions that we ask) in the mystery of God's own sovereign purpose. God loves you because he loves you, and that is that. In Paul's thought too the concept of grace is contrasted, over and over again, with our lack of deserving: God's love, mercy and favour are always given despite our unworthiness. Echoing the passage we saw earlier in Deuteronomy 6, Paul teaches that, 'He chose the lowly things of this world and the despised things – and the things that are not – to nullify the things that are, so that no-one may boast before him . . . Therefore, as it is written: "Let him who boasts boast in the Lord."' (1 Corinthians 1:28–31).

He loves us and so we are (counted as) worthy

God doesn't love us because we are worthy; he loves us *and so* we are counted as worthy. It's a subtle but important difference. He gave his only Son as the substitute for our sin. At the cross our sins are forgiven and our status is transformed. For those of us who accept his offer of grace, he makes us 'children of light' and adopts us as his own sons and daughters. We have been scrubbed clean, and he will plunder the universe to bring good things into the lives of his children. Nothing will ever separate us from the passionate love that binds him to us in solemn covenant. We are worth something to him! But here is the rub: we are worth something to him because, in his love, he *counts us as worthy*.

It's all about me, I mean . . . er . . . you

This subtle difference is important because it shapes the way we need to respond to his love. When we think that God loves us *because we are worth it*, there's a danger that we will turn back in on ourselves. 'If God loves me so much then, hey, that means I'm pretty important! Eat your heart out secular boosterism because you'll never match this. You can't get any higher in the "being-loved" stakes than the Creator of the universe. Wow, I'm speeeeecial!' And so the gospel gets hijacked in the service of what author Dick Keyes calls 'rear-view-mirrorism'.[3]

In rear-view-mirrorism the focus is on *how I am feeling right now*. We spend more time looking in the rear-view mirror, checking on our feelings, evaluating our image and comparing ourselves with others, than looking where we are going. As a result, life is a roller-coaster of anxious self-absorption, experiencing prideful self-satisfaction when we match up and woeful inadequacy and shame when we don't. As Keyes observes, rather than simply worshipping God, in rear-view-mirrorism we ask, 'What sort of experience of worship I am having – how is this making me feel? How am I feeling as I pray today?'[4] C. S. Lewis compared this to pulling up a plant each day to check the roots, just to be sure that everything is progressing satisfactorily.[5] But 'getting' that God loves us because he loves us and not because of our intrinsic 'worthiness' prompts a quite different kind of response: we are amazed by grace and not by ourselves. This kind of response is externalizing and outward-looking, not internalized and self-absorbed.

Amazed by grace

In Luke's Gospel we read that the angel visited Mary with the momentous news: 'Greetings, you who are highly favoured! The Lord is with you' (Luke 1:26–38, 46–55). Now look carefully at how Mary responds. Notice first that there is no indication here that Mary believes that she has been chosen because of any particular worthiness in herself. In fact, we read that she is 'greatly troubled' and perplexed about being addressed in such exalted terms.[6] The Greek word translated 'found favour' is equivalent to a common phrase that was used in the calling of many of the great Old Testament heroes who were also on the receiving end of God's grace. Noah, for example, 'found favour in the eyes of the LORD' in the face of the gathering storm (Genesis 6:8). Gideon asked whether he 'had found favour' in the eyes of the Lord (Judges 6:17) and discovered the answer when he was granted his 'sign'. David wondered whether he had 'found favour' in the eyes of the Lord, so that he might be allowed to see the ark of the covenant one more time (2 Samuel 15:25). The stress is on the free choice of God who favours particular men and women, for reasons hidden in the mystery of his purpose, rather than any particular acceptability on their part.[7]

Mary's perplexity stems from the fact that she, a young girl, has been chosen in precisely the same manner as the 'great men' of the Old Testament. She is 'deeply troubled' because *it doesn't make sense*. Of course, she will be even more 'troubled' by the impending news that she is going to give birth to a son. But her perplexity right now precedes that news. It's anchored in the reality that she, an ordinary teenage girl in an ordinary home on an ordinary afternoon, has 'found favour with God'.

But secondly, notice how Mary responds to the news:

My soul glorifies the Lord
    and my spirit rejoices in God my Saviour,
for he has been mindful
    of the humble state of his servant.
(Luke 1:46–48)

She doesn't gush, 'Well, that makes me special!' or 'Hey, to God I'm big stuff!' There's no 'rear-view-mirrorism' here. When an ordinary life is invaded by the glory and grace of God, the only appropriate response is perplexity, awe and worship. Mary clearly felt incredibly 'special' at that moment, but her confidence was rooted in the grace of God who had been 'mindful' of her, and this is expressed in self-forgetful praise. Our response to being touched by grace must similarly be outward, not inward. God is not a 'theological means to a psychological end'.[8] Grace is the antidote to 'rear-view-mirrorism'.

Think biblically about yourself

OK, so how should this affect the way that we think about ourselves? How do we tackle feelings of inferiority, lack of confidence and 'image' consciousness, however they may have been caused? Being *counted as worthy* by God, loved and redeemed by him, carries positive messages about how we should think about ourselves. As we saw earlier, even in our fallen state when under God's judgment, human beings are called to treat one another with dignity – thus, all human life is sacred and the foundation doctrines of creation set high standards for the sanctity of human life and for mutual honour and respect. This has big implications for social ethics and underpins the central call in Christian belief to compassion and service of other people.

Further, as we shall see, the reality of God's grace should revolutionize the way we think about our gifts and the contribution we are called to make to God's world and to building his kingdom. The issue of our 'worth' has been settled once and for all at the cross; nothing will ever separate us from the love of a God who counts us as worthy. But despite these truths, the Bible steers us away from a preoccupation with valuing ourselves and trying to nurture positive feelings about our worth. Instead it calls us to accept and embrace our new identity as God's children, lift our sights to a story that is bigger than ourselves, and *stop judging and evaluating ourselves altogether.*

Shifting focus

As we have seen, the problem with worrying about 'worth' is that you never know how much is 'enough'. It would be nice to be able to rustle up non-contingent self-esteem, that is, a sort of inner sense of self-'worth' that stands independently of how we behave, or how we compare, but in reality trying to 'feel good' about ourselves tends to accentuate rather than cure our insecurities. This is because, as hard as we try not to worry about what other people think, the effort to feel positive simply drives us back to the same old habits of making comparisons and trying to win approval.

The answer is to stop judging, 'rating' or scoring yourself *as a person* altogether. Stop trying to label yourself as 'good' or 'bad', 'worthy' or 'worthless'. Instead embrace and accept your biblical identity – how God in his grace now sees and understands you. As we shall see later, you *do* need to judge or evaluate your individual attributes, such as your ability to play the trumpet, run a mums' group efficiently or lead a Bible study group. And we certainly need to judge and evaluate individual acts of sin and discern the motives that underlie them. But it's time to bring an end to evaluating or 'rating' yourself as a human being. God has done that for you. Because of his gift of grace, you are loved, blessed and called into his glory. And that's that.

I do not even judge myself

Let's see how this worked in the early church. Reading over the early chapters of Paul's first letter to the Corinthians, we discover a congregation riddled with quarrelling and rivalry. By linking themselves with 'big-name' apostles and teachers, the Corinthians were playing at being 'cool by association': 'I am of Paul!' or 'So what? I am of Apollos!' To deal with this, Paul fields two powerful arguments.

First, he tells them to stop caring about what other people think of them. They need to lift their sights and change their perspective. We are all part of something bigger than ourselves, he says, including your favourite apostolic celebrities: 'What, after all, is Apollos? And what is Paul? Only servants, through whom you came to believe – as the Lord has assigned to each his task. I planted the seed, Apollos watered it, but God made it grow' (3:5–6).

Do you see what Paul is saying here? We are guests of a greater reality: you may have been given one job and I may have been assigned another, but we are all serving a higher purpose. It's not about our own prestige or self-aggrandizement. And it's certainly not about rank and status. The implication is clear. You don't need to 'big yourself up'. You don't have to sweat over your rank, recognition and status. God is in charge of handing out the different jobs and positions. Paul's big message is that we are all equally dependent on God, so stop caring about what people think about you. He goes on to model this powerfully when, in response to smears about his own apostleship, he asserts, 'I care very little if I am judged by you or by any human court' (1 Corinthians 4: 3).

So far so good. As the author and pastor Tim Keller[9] points out, there are few counsellors, Christian or otherwise, who would disagree with Paul's first point. You need to stop caring about how other people rank and assess you, because it's God who hands out these different callings and we are all accountable to him.

But now look at Paul's second big message: ' . . . I do not even judge myself' (4:3). Here, says Keller, comes the point of divergence with much secular (and Christian) psychology: 'Many counsellors . . . [go on to insist that] . . . the only thing that should concern me is what I think about me. It is not about other people's standards. I should only mind about what I think my standards should be. I should choose my own standards. So the counsellors' advice is, "Decide who you want to be and then be it" because it only matters what you think of yourself.'[10]

In fairness, when counsellors use phrases like this, they don't necessarily mean that it's only our own values and standards that matter. They may be trying to help their client see that they can't go on relying upon other people to make up their minds for them. You can't decide what's right or wrong simply by tuning in to the nearest person and taking your cue from them. Counsellors may be saying that 'you have to decide for yourself'. You have to take responsibility for handling your emotions and thoughts. In this sense, too, God confronts us with a responsibility to make up our own minds: 'Choose . . . this day whom you will serve' (Joshua 24:15).

But Keller is surely right when he insists that many counsellors go beyond this to assert that not only do we have to make up our minds, we have to make up our 'value' as well. 'It's what I think about myself that counts. I decide my self-worth and value and I don't care what other people think.' But Paul's second point takes us in a completely different direction. When he says, 'I do not even judge myself', he is saying, 'I don't care what you think and, you know, I don't care what I think.' Paul is out of the business of self-evaluation altogether. He has stopped the treadmill and decided to get off.

Stop judging yourself. A first glance at 1 Corinthians 4:4 might lead you to think that Paul is saying that he personally doesn't need to worry about judgment because his 'conscience is clear . . . ' But look carefully at what comes next: ' . . . but that does not make me innocent.' Paul knows that conscience can mislead us and it's hard to discern the mixed motives that underlie our best efforts. So he doesn't look to his conscience to acquit him and he certainly doesn't look to the Corinthians who have placed themselves in judgment over him. The reason? The only judgment that matters for Paul is the judgment of God: 'It is the Lord who judges me' (verse 4).

In the dock

There are two senses to 'being judged' by God here. The immediate matter under judgment as far as the Corinthian Christians are concerned is Paul's performance as an apostle and teacher. Paul recognizes that the bar is set high for servants of the gospel; faithfulness counts, and we are all accountable for what we do with the gifts that God entrusts to us. But the Corinthians are not going to sit on the judge's bench. And neither is Paul. The only judgment about stewardship, the only 'well done' that matters to Paul is the one that comes from God. So Paul refuses to rank himself by what they think or by what he thinks. He is just going to get on with the job.

But if we consider the entire context of these verses, there's a second 'deeper' sense of judgment in here too. When Paul attacks the Corinthian Christians' competitiveness and ranking behaviours, he shows them, over and over again, that *they are seeking something that they already have*: love, approval, significance and calling. They have it in spades. 'All things are yours,' announces Paul, ' . . . the world or life or death or the present or the future'. How come? Because 'you are of Christ and Christ is of God' (3:23).

So we see that, in this wider context, the verdict is in on the only judgment that counts. Jesus takes our stand in the dock and dies our death. God looks on his Son and counts his perfect life as though it were ours. And now, there is no condemnation for those who are 'in Christ Jesus' (Romans 8:1). On this basis, Paul doesn't care what the Corinthians think and he doesn't care what he thinks. The verdict (as Tim Keller says) has already been handed down. He is a loved and forgiven child of God. So he refuses even to judge himself.

So stop judging yourself

Let me tell you about Stephen. Stephen could be a male model. He's good looking, has a carefully honed six-pack and, superficially, he oozes the natural confidence to go with it. People are attracted to him, he's friendly and outgoing and, whatever the situation, without really trying, Stephen seems to bubble up to become the centre of attention. They say he's a 'born leader'. But one afternoon on a long stroll during a conference, Stephen told me about a different reality of emotions that lurked inside.

Much of that natural charm, I learned, had been generated by the fact that Stephen had been an only child. Indeed, his parents had been told that they would never have children, so when he appeared out of the blue, he was seen as an ultra-special living miracle – and treated as such. Chauffeuring him daily with a little triangle in the rear window, 'Prince on board', Stephen's parents scrimped and saved to send him to the best schools. Because their son was special to them, they fell into the fantasy that he must be special to everybody, and they began to script his life accordingly.

The family belonged to a small church where it was relatively easy to stand out among the few other children. When he was aged about twelve, a well-meaning but misguided old lady came over to him and asked for his full name, so that she could write it carefully in her diary. 'What's that for?' asked Stephen. 'Well, we are going to be hearing much more about you in the future, young man,' she said. 'There's something special; I can see it . . .'

Almost effortlessly, Stephen gained a degree at Cambridge University and, much to his parents' delight, was soon president of the Christian Union. He only just missed a blue in rowing. And now, as we walked along the seashore, he's still the guy that everybody wants to invite to the party. On the face of it, Stephen has it all.

But as we talked that afternoon, I learned that Stephen struggled with powerful feelings of insecurity, complicated by a brooding anger. For all his natural ability to attract attention and gain recognition, rather than feeling truly himself, Stephen still felt like a fake extension of his parents' dreams and aspirations. He had grown to hate the way they boasted of his achievements to friends. Like Benjamin in the classic movie *The Graduate*, when he left university, he was soon made aware what *everybody else* wanted for his life, but he didn't know what *he* wanted. Feeling almost programmed by his parents' expectations, he was held captive to 'being special' while, at the same time, plagued with fear that at any moment – like the emperor found wearing no clothes – he too would be caught out as being just plain old ordinary.

How would you try to help Stephen? As we saw earlier, most counsellors would tell him that he needs to work through his anger, explore his relationship with his parents further, detach himself from their and others' expectations, and work out for himself what he wants from his life. So far so good. But many would suggest, or guide the conversation in the direction, that Stephen needs to learn to value himself 'as a person'. That afternoon I tried to offer a more radical and far-reaching suggestion. I explored the possibility of stopping thinking about his importance and 'worth' altogether and, instead, concentrating on living out what it truly means to be God's loved child.

Relatively brief chats like this rarely produce radical results, and we mustn't fall into the trap of simplistic solutions again. But I tell this story because, for Stephen, that afternoon something definitely 'clicked'. Yes, he needed to talk through his anger and ventilate some of those feelings. And yes, it coincided with powerful ministry at the conference about the freely given grace of God. But the idea of stopping judging yourself altogether fired his imagination. He left the conference with a new-found commitment to getting out of the self-judgment business altogether.

The self-esteem treadmill: time to get off

Do you remember the psychologist Albert Ellis's argument against self-esteem that we considered in chapter 8? As a secularist, Ellis argues that self-esteem ideology is a philosophical vacuum. If you think about it, says Ellis, you are composed of hundreds, thousands of individual traits that result in a variety of actions, some good and some bad. It's illogical to try to decorate yourself with an 'averaged-out' rating of your overall 'worth'. So, Ellis says, 'Stop judging yourself as a person.' Instead of attempting to arrive at an overall global score, confine yourself to rating and judging individual behaviours and stop rating *yourself* altogether. Otherwise we find ourselves trying to boost self-worth with the sort of ranking behaviours that Paul sees in Corinth. Stop worrying about your value and meaning and just accept yourself, says Ellis.

But, outside of God's grace, can you 'just accept yourself'? Ellis's argument (as a secularist) is fine, provided there is no Judge and no judgment. But if there is a supreme Judge who holds us accountable, then it's a fantasy. At the 'appointed time,' says Paul, the Lord 'will bring to light what is hidden in darkness and will expose the motives of men's hearts' (1 Corinthians 4:5). There is no foundation for simply 'accepting yourself' in the face of the judgment of God. We need to know, and then to accept, his free offer of grace.

For those who are 'in Christ', however, Ellis's suggestion *does* work. Your identity in him is settled once and for all. There is no future salvation judgment for those who have been adopted as children of God. We need to reject globalizing from the specific ('Hey, I'm a great footballer') to the general (Wow, then I'm a great person), both because it's illogical and because the verdict is already in. We are loved children of God and nothing we think, do or say can alter that. So accept your identity as a loved child of God and lift your sights to serve his glory.

Be compassionate towards yourself

As we travel the road to self-forgetfulness and human flourishing, how do we combat rebel emotions and thoughts that threaten to drag us back into self-condemnation and shame? How do we tackle desires to impress and perform that simply refuse to 'go away'?

For moral lapses there is the joy of confession and the forgiveness of a loving Father. But how do we respond to those persisting weaknesses of character and painful emotions, which may have their roots in the past and in 'sin done to us'? How do we deal with issues of temperament and disposition? In the next chapter we will learn how to dispute with thoughts and attitudes so that our self-understanding is brought into line with our identity in Christ as God's loved children. But as we make this journey, I suggest, we need to show ourselves the same *compassion and kindness* that God shows us as our Father.

Showing compassion towards yourself is different from esteeming yourself. Self-esteem ideology encourages us to respond to weakness and failure by accentuating the positive and affirming the good. It keeps us focused on *evaluation*, thriving when the reviews are good, but getting snagged in disappointed introspection or denial when they are bad. In contrast, showing ourselves compassion embraces the full reality of our imperfections, but says 'go easy' as we do so. After all, God has compassion on us – he 'remembers that we are dust' (Psalm 103:14). Rather than punishing ourselves harshly when we fail, or pitting ourselves against others, trying to prove we are better in endless games of comparison, we need to show ourselves the same kindness, patience and forbearance that God shows us. C. S. Lewis put it like this:

> But if you are a poor creature – poisoned by a wretched upbringing in some house full of vulgar jealousies and senseless quarrels – saddled, by no choice of your own, with some loathsome sexual perversion – nagged day in and day out by an inferiority complex that makes you snap at your best friends – do not despair. He knows all about it. You are one of the poor whom He blessed. He knows what a wretched machine you are trying to drive. Keep on. Do what you can. One day (perhaps in another world, but perhaps far sooner than that) He will fling it on the scrap-heap and give you a new one. And then you may astonish us all – not least yourself: for you have learned your driving in a hard school . . .[11]

I am not attempting to launch a 'biblical self-compassion' movement that risks refocusing the self back onto itself. But as we travel the road to self-forgetfulness, there is important and far-reaching 'heart-work' that needs to be done in the 'here and now', and the tone of that work needs to be consistent with the compassion and kindness that God, in his grace, shows towards us as a Father.

In secular psychology, the motivation for self-compassion is usually portrayed as our own happiness and well-being.[12] Thus, it is marketed as a 'better and more effective path to happiness'.[13] Biblically consistent self-compassion, on the other hand, serves a different goal: the glory of God and the pursuit of his kingdom. To this way of thinking, compassion shown towards yourself is one component, one aspect, of pursuing something larger than 'what's good for me'. In the Sermon on the Mount, remember, Jesus picks up on his disciples' worries about who was going to pay for food and clothes. He reminds them that God counts them as worthy of his love and compassion (Matthew 6:26) and he knows that they need these things (verse 32). But then, notice how Jesus refocuses their minds away from meeting their own needs to a much larger goal: 'But seek first his kingdom and his righteousness, and all these things will be given to you as well' (verse 33). Do you see what Jesus is saying here? Your needs are not unimportant, but they must be addressed as one component of a much larger purpose – the growth of righteousness, the compassionate outward-looking building of God's kingdom and the pursuit of his glory.

Finally, this kind of self-compassion is transformative. It doesn't seek our short-term well-being but our long-term glorification. It isn't about self-pity and self-indulgence; it's about self-denial, self-discipline and self-control. And, most important of all, it is built on the gospel foundation of freedom from self-condemnation. But what does all of this look like in more practical terms? How can we begin to put some of these ideas into practice?

11. HOW TO STOP JUDGING YOURSELF

There's a hilarious sketch going around on the internet, in which a psychiatrist, played by the American actor and comedian Bob Newhart, tells his clients that they just need to 'stop it!'[1] Whatever the problem, however deeply rooted or far-reaching it may be, no matter how depressed, anxious or generally upset they may feel, for just a handful of dollars this psychiatrist tells his clients that they just need to 'stop it!' If they don't get it the first time, he ups the volume for the second time: 'Stop it!' It's a clever piece that makes an important point. But there's a danger too that it might also miss the point. Sometimes the solution really is that we need to stop doing something.

Change isn't easy. Negative thoughts and attitudes about ourselves may have been hewn out of years of corrosive family ordeals and other painful adversity. As we accumulate experience and respond to life's challenges, our reactions become embedded in vast networks of interconnected beliefs about how the world works. Over time these beliefs cohere and consolidate into something that Scripture calls 'attitudes of the heart' (Hebrews 4:12), or what psychologists call 'cognitive schema'. These are the undercurrents of the heart: 'ways of looking at the world' that shape the way we respond to it.

You've got attitude

A 'glass-half-empty' sort of person has a radically different attitude of heart to a 'glass-half-full' sort of person. This is a worn-out platitude, I know, but it's still a powerful metaphor for the way the heart *works*. On both counts, the position of the water in the glass is precisely the same, but one person sees the glass in terms of what's missing and the other in terms of what's there. 'Glass-half-empty' people tend to filter in negative information and weigh it up pessimistically: 'It may have worked last time, but this team is nowhere up to speed compared with then'; 'We're falling behind again; what did I tell you?' These are expressions of an underlying network of conviction about the fundamentally negative trajectory of the world. And with the latest brain-imaging techniques, scientists can even picture the neural networks that appear to strengthen in the brain as we practise these attitudes of the heart.[2]

The 'attitudes of the heart' that we hold about our own status and standing in the world are especially important. So a child brought up in an atmosphere of constant criticism and derision will likely form a negative, self-blaming heart attitude along the lines of: 'I'm no good; nobody wants me'; 'Might as well give up trying; I'll never win'; 'What's the use, because everybody hates me anyway.' Psychologists sometimes use the word 'mindset' for these inner patterns of thoughts and feelings, because, over time, they gradually become 'fixed' or 'set' like jelly. That is why the Bible so often warns us about 'hardness of heart'. Once we get stuck in a mould, basic heart attitudes get wired in and become impossibly difficult to shift. As somebody once put it, 'Watch your thoughts; they become words. Watch your words; they become actions. Watch your actions; they become habits. Watch your habits; they become character. Watch your character; it becomes your destiny.'

Changing attitude

So it's not easy to change the way you think. Before we can change our thoughts, we need to make the effort to tease them out and understand them. And it can sometimes take patience, effort and considerable pastoral or counselling skill to unravel the hidden secrets of the heart. Those of us who have spent time with damaged and abused individuals know just how cleverly the human mind can bury or mask painful feelings and thoughts. While we wouldn't wish to endorse the materialistic (in the case of Freud) and mystical (in the case of Jung) worldviews of the early psychoanalytic thinkers we met in chapter 1, they were clearly onto something when they talked about the mechanisms by which the mind attempts to protect itself from reality.

Furthermore, as part of this process, it can be extremely difficult to 'accept ourselves'. Dark and unpalatable aspects of your own psyche can be hard to acknowledge. That is why we often try to shuffle them off or, worse, deny them altogether. But it's not possible to deal with an issue or tackle a problem unless and until we have accepted that it is *there*. In that sense, we all need to 'accept' ourselves.

If our experience of self is riddled with self-hatred, kindled in a deprived and chaotic childhood, then it will be difficult to believe, let alone feel, that God loves and accepts us. And so here too the love and acceptance of a skilled pastor or counsellor, and the support of friends, church and home fellowship group, can be crucially important in the process of moving us to the point where we can allow ourselves to experience love, forgiveness and acceptance as God's children.

But no matter how our hearts have been damaged, sooner or later God's love draws us back to the challenge of heart change. And, given the power of emotions such as guilt and shame, and the strength of our instincts for approval and recognition, the call to stop judging ourselves is one of the most important challenges we shall ever face. In fact this task is at the very heart of Christian growth and formation. So for the rest of this chapter we are going to drill down to the practicalities. When we find ourselves lapsing into self-judgment and condemnation, how can we learn to *stop it!*?

Learning to dispute with yourself

The Protestant Reformation was born in disputation. In fact, Martin Luther's famous 'Ninety-Five Theses', nailed to the door of the Castle Church in Wittenberg, were originally entitled 'Disputation of Martin Luther on the Power and Efficacy of Indulgences'. Because of the drama involved, I have always thought of the ninety-five theses as a quick-fire manifesto with a 'cut-and-thrust' style. But it was actually more an invitation to public scholarly debate, written in a searching, rather than dogmatic, format.[3] By adopting this style, Luther was following in a centuries-old tradition of public disputation: searching debate that carefully clarifies the arguments and then, from opposing points of view, sifts, weighs and critiques them. Public disputation has played a crucial role in the formation of Christian thought throughout much of its history. But, for the Christian who wants to grow, the most important disputation is the one we need to have with *ourselves*.

In modern psychology the ancient art of disputing has been carried over in the work of Martin Seligman and Albert Ellis. Seligman argues that,

Although most adults and children are naturally skilled disputers when accused by someone else, we are poor disputers when we are our own accusers. We know that others' opinions of us can be biased and wrong, yet we treat our own opinions of ourselves as indisputable. Self-disputing is a lasting and effective way to challenge the validity of unrealistic expectations.[4]

Our heads are full of junk that we find hard to challenge. Some of these irrational thoughts and attitudes have been put there by other people; others, like viruses, we've caught from the world around us; and some we've simply made up for ourselves. Of course, the Christian believer holds that the secular mind teems with irrationality, ranging from idolatry to the delusions of self-invention. But despite having been given a 'new heart', Christians harbour plenty of junk too: false thoughts about the world, inflexible beliefs about themselves, and hopelessly inaccurate predictions about their future. Let me give some examples.

Tom, a budding Christian musician, came to see me one day, in deep conflict about his behaviour towards his children. Having lost his temper on a couple of occasions, he was becoming increasingly preoccupied with the fear that one day he would completely lose control and cause one of his children real harm. This fear had become so intense that he was thinking of withdrawing from ministry altogether. As Tom told his story, it seemed to me that the strength of his emotions was barely different from what most hassled parents feel from time to time. And yet Tom remained convinced that this was all going to spin out of control and that one day he would do real damage and be put out of ministry altogether.

Where were these voices coming from? It turned out that Tom had been brutally beaten by his father and had never properly talked about his emotions or his past. His anxiety about the dangerous and unpredictable world of emotion led to his being a relatively 'closed' and over-controlled teenager. And then, growing into adulthood, even fairly normal anger and frustration could trigger a crippling fear that (as his mother always predicted) he would one day *'turn out just like his father'*.

June's problem, on the other hand, was that she didn't feel 'really good' at anything; friends thought of her as something of a 'gloom-and-doom merchant'. This was puzzling, because clearly she was a competent mother, an outstanding hostess and a popular part-time nurse. So why did June harbour the belief that she was 'just no good'? Where did this particular storyline have its beginning?

It turned out that June had had a very difficult relationship with her mother. 'I always felt like an athlete competing in the high jump,' she said. 'As far as my mother was concerned, no matter how well I did or how hard I tried, the bar was always moved higher – until I failed.' This was the story she now lived by. And when she did fail, she could almost hear her mother's mocking in her ears: 'Told you so!'

June expected to fail. She lacked confidence, felt out of place socially and, over the previous year or so, had developed a tendency towards chronic tiredness. She attended church and was part of a home group in which others had tried gently to help her challenge her fixed beliefs. And after seeing a counsellor, she had even developed an insightful understanding about the malign influence her mother held over her. But she couldn't seem to make progress in changing her thoughts. June's mind continued to be dominated by the story woven out of the legacy of the past.

James was a sensitive personality, with a strong tendency to ruminate over his sins and shortcomings. When he made a mistake or fell into sin, the guilt that stacked up could haunt him for days on end. His storyline was replete with words like 'always', 'never' and 'completely': 'I'm always messing up'; 'I'll never get the hang of this'; 'I'm a complete idiot.' And when he fell into sin, he thought that God's grace and love had deserted him like rats off a sinking ship. Because he had done a *wicked thing*, you see, James believed that he was a *wicked person*.

William, on the other hand, spent hours at the gym and, to his delight, had developed a particularly fine six-pack. With more than a hint of smugness, William quietly noted the beer-bellies and love-handles growing on friends around him. He liked to catch sight of his biceps and well-shaped torso in the nicely placed mirror in the men's locker room. And, as he checked out the other guys, he felt himself moving quietly up the pecking order. Because William has a better six-pack, you see, he thought he was a better person . . .

I hope that you can spot the 'junk thinking' rattling around these scenarios. To grow into our status as loved children of God, we need to be 'transformed by the renewing of our minds' (Romans 12:2). In other words, because the mind is the originator of these irrational thoughts, and the arena in which they get played out, this is where they have to be challenged and beaten. Disputation is the art of putting your thoughts to the test. We clarify what they are saying and submit them to a court of inquiry. Does this add up? Where is this coming from? If I examine them objectively, what are these thoughts actually saying? And are they *true*?

Touching truth

The most important touchstone in the matter of truth of course is God's Word. 'For the word of God is living and active. Sharper than any double-edged sword, it penetrates even to dividing soul and spirit, joints and marrow; it judges the thoughts and attitudes of the heart' (Hebrews 4:12). Here is truth that challenges our fictional beliefs about God, and truth capable of disrupting the fictions we hold about ourselves. So, Paul said, 'We take captive every thought to make it obedient to Christ' (2 Corinthians 10:5). Of course, the notion of Scripture as a double-edged sword and ideas about 'making thoughts captive to God's word' are common currency among evangelical Christians. For Bible learners it rings all the right bells, and for Bible teachers it rolls off the tongue with heart-warming ease. We can all nod with approval to this one. Provided, that is, we don't actually have to do anything about it.

And here is the rub. Committing to the long, painful, effortful process of changing the way we think is hard work. A common deception is to assume that, because we agree with a particular proposition, our work is over. Wrong. It hasn't even begun. Habits of a lifetime don't just roll over and die. Another common form of self-deception is to think, like June in the vignette above, that, because we have confided in somebody and gained insight into the story behind our problem, the job is done. I play this trick on myself all the time. I impress people with my insights and self-awareness, but then do nothing about it. But talking about a problem rarely changes anything. And reading this won't change anything either; nobody gets up out of an armchair changed after merely reading a book.

Do you want to change?

So do you really *want* to change? This is perhaps the most important question a skilled pastor can ask. Change is hard because it involves a journey into uncharted territory. It commits us to sustained effort and opens up the risk of disappointment and setback. And so, sadly, when faced with these realities, countless numbers of people who seek help eventually decide (without really admitting it to themselves) that they would rather stick with what they have got.

Change involves a commitment to the long haul. You have to be prepared to do something once and then to do it again. It involves sustained effort and a lot of practice. But if you really want to, and if you are prepared to do it, you can make a start today on tackling some of the junk that clutters your skull. You don't have to accept passively the put-downs and insults you fling at yourself; you don't have to go on living out the toxic life-scripts that others have left in your head; and you don't have to buy into your own grand delusions.

How does this work? In the same way that we dispute with the cashier when she presents us with the wrong bill, we need to learn to dispute with our thoughts when they present us with the wrong facts. The first stage is to take a step back and put them under the spotlight. Check your facts. Weigh your thoughts carefully. Share them with a friend. Let the light of the gospel question their validity and truthfulness. And where a thought is illogical, you need to refute it. Let's see how this could work in practice.

Disputing a globalizing mindset

Welcome to the world of globalization. Globalization is a thinking error committed by people who jump from the specific to the general: because I committed a *specific sin*, that makes me an all-round *sinful, wicked person*; because I made *a bad mistake*, I must be a *bad person*. As William's six-pack reminds us, it works the other way too: because I am a great athlete, an opera superstar or a brilliant preacher, this makes me a great *person*.

We are all instinctive globalizers. Rather than accepting our status as loved children of God, we stake our significance on a specific gift or weakness, or upon the last thing that we did. We globalize from sinful acts and thoughts, and from individual strengths and weaknesses. It works slightly differently in the area of *moral* strengths and shortcomings (sinful acts and thoughts) compared with *competence* strengths and shortcomings (character weaknesses and gifting), so I am going to deal with these separately.

Worst of sinners or child of God?

Thoughts that follow sinful acts are particularly troublesome to dispute with, because guilt and shame are powerful emotions, and we find it difficult to accept the full implications of God's great gift of grace. In the case of sinful acts on the part of a *non-Christian*, globalizing instincts are (in a theological sense) actually quite accurate. A specific sin is indeed the fruit of the global grip of sin on the human soul. As we saw in chapter 9, we sin because we are 'in sin'. By the standards that God set us, or indeed the standards we ourselves set for other people, we have 'fallen short' of God's glory. The verdict is in. We can't perform our way out of this reality with clever deeds or scrupulous acts of righteousness. As the apostle Paul put it, 'Christ Jesus came into the world to save sinners – of whom I am the worst' (1 Timothy 1:15). He meant that when a man or a woman comes under conviction about their sin, it can be hard to imagine anybody worse. It's a subjective rather than an objective judgment, but that is how it can feel.

This state of affairs has been radically reversed for the loved child of God. True, we continue to commit individual sins: 'If we claim to be without sin, we deceive ourselves and the truth is not in us' (1 John 1:8). But whether we consider ourselves to have been the 'worst of sinners' like Paul or just a good old-fashioned, all-round sinner like everybody else, 'sinner' no longer defines our status in Christ. Our standing in the eyes of God has undergone a radical transformation: we are loved children of God.

We are called to weave this new language of status into every facet of our lived experience, including our acts of sin. This means that, when we commit sins, we do so as loved children of God. Our identity doesn't change. But the problem we face is that guilt and shame try to propel us backwards into the old global sense of sin and wickedness: we feel that God has fled from us in disgust; we tell ourselves that he has put us out of his household; we convince ourselves that we no longer *belong*. As instinctive globalizers, we say, 'Because I have done this thing, I am a corrupted, worthless, unimportant piece of garbage who no longer deserves to be called God's child.'

But even in his darkest moments of sin and corruption, the Christian who has grasped grace refuses to allow this verdict to linger. No matter how far we have strayed, the significance, favour, worth and ultimate destiny that flow from our core identity as God's child need to be defended with a clear, bold, assertive and specific 'No!' Although I have committed this sin, sin no longer defines my significance or status. I am a loved, secure and significant child of God – who has sinned.

Now, of course, this truth doesn't make specific sins any less serious or damaging. In many respects, the reality that we sin as a loved son or daughter of God should intensify the pain. That is why Paul warns the Corinthians about the incongruous harm of immorality to their spiritual well-being: 'Shall I then take the members of Christ and unite them with a prostitute? Never!' (1 Corinthians 6:15). Neither does this truth wipe out the consequences of sin that may have to be shouldered for years to come. But despite these realities, in moments of shameful darkness *more than at any other time*, we are called to assert our status as God's beloved child.

And we need to say, 'No!' to self-accusing thoughts that tell us otherwise.

Superman or omni-shambles?

Let's think now about skills and gifts. We are instinctive global-izers in these areas too: 'I am a brilliant cook, so that makes me a great person'; 'I always get picked last for the school team, so that makes me an unimportant, insignificant person'; 'I've got about half the Facebook "friend requests" of everybody else, so that means I'm a pretty worthless person.'

We don't often allow thoughts that are such obvious junk to form fully at a conscious level. More often than not, they make their presence felt through our emotions. We notice, for example, that performing well and getting praise and attention from others makes us 'feel good'. The feel-good factor after a big achievement can have all the force and intoxi-cating pleasure of a narcotics fix. So we do it again. 'Feeling bad' after a piece of negative feedback, on the other hand, can torpedo our confidence and energy for weeks on end.

But globalizing from specific gifts and skills to making global judgments about our significance and status as a person is profoundly illogical. We are each unique individuals, with hundreds of different gifts, skills and achievements. Every one of them is capable of being evaluated separately and given a secret mental score. Amy, for example, may be much admired in her legal practice for her ability to sift arguments and advocate her clients' cases before a judge. In everybody's view she scores highly in that area. But if they had the choice, nobody would ever want to sample Amy's cooking. On the other hand, she may be a wonderfully thoughtful daughter. But then in several areas she isn't always a particularly competent mother. She may bring group Bible studies to life with her insights, but her prayer life is an undisciplined shambles. Which of these individual 'scores' should she choose to generate her overall score or 'value' and then judge herself? Does she pick the positives and ignore the negatives, or should she work out an average? Or maybe she should just go with the last one that occurred? Of course not. Instead Amy needs to stop trying to score, evaluate and rate herself *as a person* altogether.

Stop it!

But how? Take the example of a pastor called Nick. One fine Sunday morning, as he stands at the door shaking hands, he receives several positive compliments about his sermon. In his heart Nick judges that it was indeed a pretty good talk, and he's grateful for the feedback that confirms it. As a result, Nick forms the 'sober judgment' (Romans 12:3) that, although he still has much to learn, God has gifted him as a Bible teacher. But then, as he walks home for his Sunday lunch, Nick spots in himself a globalizing instinct that tells him that, because he is a very good preacher, he is also a very important and significant person. What should he to do?

Nick has a simple mental trick up his sleeve. Whenever he gets good feedback about his preaching, he has a small 'statement' that he rehearses in his head to himself: 'This person may think I'm a good preacher, but they don't know what kind of a husband I am, how well I engage with my family responsibilities and how much attention I pay to my prayer life. So I refuse to stake my significance on this particular achievement or on the praises and criticisms of other people. I accept myself as a loved child of God. I am gradually breaking free of the endless pursuit of "judging" and "scoring" myself altogether.'

You can develop similar mental tricks to dispute your own globalizing instincts. 'I may be a great businessman, but the

Lord knows I have a lot of work to do on my calling as a father and husband – I refuse to inflate myself in my work setting and strut around with an air of importance. I am a loved child of God, with much to learn'; 'I may have been beaten down by my mother's judgmental criticism, but I refuse to listen to that voice from the past, and I refuse to allow my mistakes and failings to reconnect me with it. The Lord sees the work I do among children and the skilled way I handle my junior staff at work. I am a loved child of God, with much to learn.'

The tone through all of this needs to be *compassionate*. This means that we show ourselves the same kindness and understanding that God show us. The psalmist wrote,

> The Lord is compassionate and gracious,
>   slow to anger, abounding in love . . .
> As a father has compassion on his children,
>   so the Lord has compassion on those who fear him;
> for he knows how we are formed,
>   he remembers that we are dust.
> (Psalm 103:8, 13–14)

God understands that we are on a journey and that it's hard going. He knows that we are formed from dust . . . that we have been dealt different genetic hands that may have saddled us with a nit-picking, judgmental temperament, or a 'nervous', self-deprecating disposition. He knows about the constant criticism of your mother or the harsh, unremitting expectations of your father. It takes time to get them out of your head. So allow God to love you, and show yourself the same patience, forbearance and compassion that he has towards you. When you face failure and struggle with your general shortcomings, work at finding ways to grow as a Christian, not because you are a hateful and unacceptable person, but because you are God's loved child and you want to build his kingdom.

Sober as a judge: how to approach your strengths and weaknesses

OK, so hopefully we grasp the need to say 'no' to globalizing. But how then should we think about our individual talents and achievements, and the scores and 'ratings' we give them? In his letter to the Romans, Paul urged his readers: 'Think of yourself with sober judgment, in accordance with the measure of faith God has given you' (12:3). We need to note the context here. Paul says that the church fellowship works like a body, with different parts having different functions: 'In Christ we who are many form one body, and each member belongs to all the others. We have different gifts, according to the grace given us' (verses 5–6). In these verses Paul isn't talking about global judgments of overall significance, but rather the mental process of sorting and sifting our gifts in terms of how they can best contribute to the building up of the church.

Paul is specifically warning against using the scores (or estimates) that we give to our individual gifts in order to boost our value and standing in the eyes of other people: 'Do not think of yourself more highly than you ought . . . Each member belongs to all the others' (verses 3, 5). Paul is saying that we have different gifts from God, for the building up of the church, so we need to use these to build the church up, and not (by globalizing them) to build ourselves up.

But Paul also urges his readers to have a clear understanding of their gifts and of the relative quality of their work. The term 'sober' conveys the meaning of accuracy and objectivity. We are urged in Scripture to be realistic both about our weaknesses *and our strengths*. This means that we can positively celebrate the gifts that we bring to God's church as having a real impact upon the growth and development of his kingdom. There is no room here for responding to our achievements with statements like, 'It wasn't me; it was the Lord' or the 'let-go-and-let-God' syndrome.

Take the example of Rob, another young minister who agonizes over his sermons. Suppose that one Sunday morning after the service a little old lady clasps him by the hand:

'You know that was the most wonderful message this morning, Vicar. Thank you so much!'

'It wasn't me,' he intones. 'It was the Lord.'

There's a glint in the little old lady's eye . . . 'It wasn't that good,' she laughs. 'The Lord would have known that Nero didn't "fiddle" while Rome burned . . . Violins hadn't even been invented then!'

Rob laughs nervously, 'Ah well, that must have been my contribution!'

This is a profoundly unbiblical view of our gifts and skills. God gets credit for the good bits, and Rob gets credits for the mistakes! But the numerous references in Scripture to our being praised by God, rewarded for our efforts and commended for our achievements demand that we view our work as having real value and real effect. Paul clearly took pleasure and legitimate 'pride' in what he achieved for God's kingdom. In his second letter to the church at Corinth (10:13–18), for example, he shows that it's possible to 'boast' (take legitimate pleasure) in our own endeavours in certain circumstances and within 'proper limits': 'We, however, will not boast beyond proper limits, but will confine our boasting to the field God has assigned to us, a field that reaches even to you.' The 'proper limits' here are the geographic boundaries of the field of work that God has assigned to him.

He is saying that he will confine his 'boasting' to the sphere of ministry to which God has appointed him and not, as some do, try to inflate his ego by making claims about other people's spheres of work.

Are you uncomfortable with the idea of 'boasting'? We need to detach ourselves from its modern connotation as inherently arrogant and self-serving. Paul's use of the term usually means to take pleasure in, to enjoy, to celebrate. Paul makes clear that it can be right and proper, notwithstanding his injunction that we should 'boast in the Lord', to express praise for, and to take pleasure in, certain aspects of *our own work for the kingdom*. In his first letter, for example, he asked the Corinthians, 'Are you not the *result of my work in the Lord*?' (1 Corinthians 9:1, emphasis mine). He describes the Christians at Thessalonica as the 'crown in which we will glory' (1 Thessalonians 2:19), and he tells the Philippians that he longs for them to 'shine like stars in the universe . . . in order that I may boast on the day of Christ that I did not labour or run for nothing' (Philippians 2:15–16).

'Boasting' today means that we use our achievements to impress others and massage our social status. Paul's concept of 'boasting' meant celebrating the thing for what it was: a good and valued gift to the work of God's kingdom. If we really understood the intense pleasure we bring to God and allowed ourselves to *feel* the pleasure of receiving his praise, we would be barely tempted to flaunt our gifts before others. 'How can you believe if you accept praise from one another, yet make no effort to obtain the praise that comes from the only God?' Jesus asked (John 5:44).

Of course, there is a paradox here. On the one hand, everything we achieve depends on our having been given a gift in the first instance, and then given the strength to use it: 'Apart from me you can do nothing,' Jesus said (John 15:5). 'Let him who boasts boast in the Lord,' said Paul (2 Corinthians 10:17). God our Creator is the ultimate source and giver of all life, including the good that we do. On the one hand, all that we have is given by God and all that we do is in his strength. And yet, on the other hand, it involves real effort, real pleasure (and sometimes pain) and real reward. We are called to live the paradox.

Would you like to enjoy the freedom of being able to serve God without it being about *me*? Do you long to give a talk, help a friend, receive a compliment or hear a word of criticism, without it being about *me*? Wouldn't you like to be honoured for something without having to battle pride, and be rebuked for something without falling into despair? Wouldn't you like to lead an outstanding summer camp for teenagers and feel genuinely that it was about building up the kingdom and not inflating your ego? Wouldn't you like to be able to beat the life out of the other football team, but feel genuine pleasure for the team members who got to score the goals you would have loved to have scored? Tim Keller puts it like this: 'The truly gospel-humble person is a self-forgetful person whose ego is just like his or her toes. It just works. It does not draw attention to itself. The toes just work; the ego just works. Neither draws attention to itself.'[5]

Do you long to 'work' like this? Then commit to the long, slow business of change; stop judging yourself and embrace your significance and status in Christ.

12. THE BIGGER-THAN-YOUR-EGO TRIP!

He must become greater; I must become less.
John the Baptist

Business was looking pretty good for John the Baptist and his disciples. From all over the country, sometimes after travelling for days and weeks on end, crowds of people were coming to be baptized. John's team had even needed to relocate to somewhere that guaranteed plenty of water to cope with the flow (John 3:23). With admirers flocking around them, John's disciples must have felt as though they ruled the world.

One day, however, after falling into an argument with a bystander, something happened that changed their minds and their world. During the course of the dispute, John's disciples learned that Jesus had also started baptizing over on the other side of the Jordan. Worse still, increasingly, people were 'going over to him' (John 3:25–26). The disciples hurried over to John to warn him about the situation. What was their problem?

Status and limited good

John's team was suffering an acute bout of *status anxiety*. Half a century ago, on the back of his work among rural peasant communities, an anthropologist called George Foster devised a theory of what he called the 'limited good'.[1] Foster taught that rural peasants, whose existence and survival depend on working their land, tend to think that everything, like the land they have to share out between themselves, is similarly in short supply. There is only so much to go around. This means that, if *you* get a bit more of it, then *I* get a bit less. Foster believed that this mode of thinking coloured and shaped his peasants' approach to just about everything else too: 'All of the desired things in life such as land, wealth, health, friendship and love, manliness and honour, respect and status, power and influence, security and safety, exist in finite quantity and are always in short supply.'[2] In the rural world of peasantry there's no 'win-win'; it's always 'win-lose'. If you get more, then I get less.

When you think about it, this insight applies well beyond the borders of rural peasant communities. Watch two children sitting on a floor littered with as many toys as they can handle, fighting over the possession of one of them. In a City of London bar feel the tense undertone of anxiety as bankers compare and boast about the size of their bonuses. Peep into the cloistered precincts of some of our great cathedrals and watch clergy clinging to their titles and struggling for power. The game of 'limited good' is being played out all around us. Indeed, it's being played out in your heart too.

So what was going on with John's disciples? As George Foster indicated, all the things we want in life, including 'honour, respect and status . . . are always in short supply';[3] there is only so much to go around. So, as people shifted over to Jesus, John's disciples felt honour, respect and status draining away from them. And they didn't like that feeling at all. From the nature of his response to them: 'He must become greater; I must become less' (John 3:30), John the

Baptist had arrived at this diagnosis also. Here was a serious case of status anxiety.

What is status anxiety?

'Status' derives from the Latin word *statum* or 'standing'. It refers to one's position in a particular social grouping or in society more generally. Technically, it tends to be used in connection with one's professional or contractual standing, but I'm more interested here in the general sense of one's value and importance in the eyes of the world. The popular philosopher Alain de Botton suggests that 'high status is thought by many (but freely admitted by few) to be one of the finest of earthly goods'.[4] The consequences of being awarded high status in a society are extremely pleasant, he says. They include resources, luxury, space, freedom and choice.

It's not so much the material and social rewards in themselves that motivate us to hunger and thirst for status, however, but the attention and deference that traditionally come with them. As Adam Smith, the Scottish father of modern economics, wrote back in 1759,

> To what purpose is all the toil and bustle of this world? What is the end of avarice and ambition, of the pursuit of wealth, of power and pre-eminence? Is it to supply the necessities of nature? The wages of the meanest labourer can supply them. What then are the advantages of that great purpose of human life which we call bettering our condition? . . . to be observed, to be attended to, to be taken notice of.[5]

Our pursuit of wealth, says Smith, is driven by a deeper, more fundamental human desire than material comforts – the longing to be observed, noticed and loved. High status brings with it a sense of being cared for and thought important too: people laugh at our jokes; they flatter us with their invitations; and they offer us deference and respect. It's an incredibly rewarding and motivating experience.

But why are we so hungry for love and attention? Because, argues Alain de Botton, we are 'afflicted by a congenital uncertainty as to our own value – as a result of which . . . our sense of identity is held captive by the judgments of those we live among'.[6] De Botton is surely right. Yes, unhappy experiences in childhood spawn insecurity and shape uncertainty as we negotiate our way in the world. But there's a deeper, 'congenital' ambiguity about our significance, woven into the human condition. As we saw in chapter 9, a sense of lostness – no longer knowing who we are and what we are for – is one of the most far-reaching consequences of sin and the human fall.

When we look inside, we discover a kaleidoscope of strengths and weaknesses, wisdom and foolishness, humour and blandness – and *we don't know how to put it all together*. And so, after gazing into empty space to ask, 'What is man . . . ?', we find ourselves looking to other people to arbitrate and settle the question for us. If we work hard enough, people will smile and offer their attention and pay us their respects. But how long before they are distracted by an altogether more enticing and entertaining offering? Here is the root of our anxiety. Status anxiety.

Pecking orders

Our fascination with hierarchy – 'pecking orders' – is an especially potent contributor to status anxiety. The higher you go, the more power you wield and the more attention you get. But the problem with pecking orders is that everybody is at it, and, if *you* move up, then *I* move down. This is why we find it so hard to see others succeed and why we take pleasure when they fail. It's why we find it so hard to offer a genuinely felt compliment. The Roman philosopher Plutarch scorned people who recognized that somebody was a better public speaker than they but couldn't bring themselves to offer a compliment, ' . . . as though commendation were money, he feels that he is robbing himself of every bit that he bestows on another'.[7] Honour, you see, is like money. It's in limited supply. So we don't like to give it away.

In the New Testament the persecution of the apostles and the early church was motivated as much by the attention they were attracting, as by genuine concerns about the content of what they were preaching (Acts 5:17; 13:45). And, as we've seen, the early church communities positively bristled with status anxiety as well: 'I follow Paul,' shouted some. 'I follow Apollos,' proclaimed the rest. The success of people 'like us' is especially hard to take. We don't mind the President of the United States living in a dream home, and most of us don't lose sleep because the Queen of England lives in Buckingham Palace. But, as Alain de Botton observes, 'If we have a pleasant home and comfortable job . . . but learn through ill-advised attendance at a school reunion that some of our old friends (there is no stronger reference group) are now living in houses larger than our own, bought on the proceeds of more enticing occupations, we are likely to return home nursing a violent sense of misfortune . . . *We envy only those whom we feel ourselves to be like*' (emphasis mine).[8] And in church life we can be surrounded by people who are very similar to us. They are in our fellowship groups, mums' groups and Sunday services. We encounter them when we make an 'ill-advised attendance' at a ministers' conference where everybody compares (subtly) the size of their congregations. There are few successes harder to stomach than those of our close friends.

John the Baptist and the status game

How do we combat status anxiety? Returning to John the Baptist and his disciples, we can see that their response to Jesus depends on a fear of 'limited good'. They are not worried about who has cornered the best spot for carrying out baptisms. This is about honour, status and importance. As people 'go over to him', Jesus is becoming *more*, and they are becoming *less*. And they don't like that feeling at all.

In our self-esteem culture we would tell them that they shouldn't think of their importance in terms of how many people they manage to baptize, but instead decide their importance for themselves. We would say that they need to learn to love themselves and stop worrying about what other people think. And in much popular Christian culture too we would follow the same knee-jerk response. Jesus, remember, wouldn't die for junk. So you just need to love and honour yourself, as he loves and respects you.

But, as we've seen, it's hard to decide your significance for yourself. We need a sense of significance that comes from beyond ourselves. That is why the Bible teaches that, in order to flourish as God intends, we need to learn how to stop judging ourselves, accept our biblical status, and live lives motivated by something greater than the pursuit of our own worth. And that is the point that John is about to make so powerfully.

Guests of a greater reality

John's counter-cultural response to his disciples carries four messages that sum up much of what I have said. First, in the great scheme of things, the only 'importance' that counts comes from God. John places the whole matter of status and honour onto an entirely different footing: 'A man can receive only what is given him from heaven . . . ' (John 3:27). Beyond all claims to importance is the reality that we possess nothing other than what we've been given by God. As D. A. Carson reminds us, God's sovereignty includes the call to specific roles and stations in life: 'For John the Baptist to have wished he were someone else, called to serve in a way many would judge more prominent . . . *he would be annulling the excellent ministry God had given him*' (emphasis mine).[9] In God's economy, importance isn't in short supply, something to be fought over. We are called to embrace the different 'stations' that God calls us to – mother, breadwinner, chief executive, pastor, preacher, house-group leader, road sweeper – as each being given by God and therefore honoured and important to him. In the abundance of God's grace there is *no limited good*. There is more than enough for everybody.

Secondly, we are all part of something bigger than ourselves. It's not about you or me. To illustrate this, John describes himself as being part of a great wedding ceremony (3:28–29). In a modern-day wedding ceremony the arrival of the bride is the moment we are all waiting for. But in the ceremony that John is talking about here, the only thing that counts is the arrival of the bridegroom. The bride 'belongs' to, and therefore serves, the glory and majesty of the bridegroom: 'The Father loves the Son and has placed everything in his hands' (3:35). We are all here to serve the glory of the bridegroom, Jesus Christ. John wants his disciples to see that it isn't about them. They may well be *at* the centre of God's purposes, but they themselves are *not the centre* of his purpose. God's purpose is to bring glory to his Son, and that is their purpose too.

Thirdly, we shouldn't use specific callings or duties given by God to puff up our own importance. At a wedding the best man doesn't compete with the bridegroom. Everybody involved – the chauffeur who drives the bride to the ceremony, the minister who takes the service, the best man who produces the ring – works together to serve a greater purpose. John doesn't need to connect his particular calling as the 'best man' heralding the arrival of the groom with his own importance. Being the best man isn't about *standing out*; it's about *fitting in*. It's not about looking inwards; it's about looking outwards in compassionate service. John has been given a role in the story, but he doesn't need to make it *his* story. John is able to judge, or 'score', the value and significance of his work, without globalizing it to judge his value and significance as a person.

Finally, *positive feelings of well-being* often accompany obedient service that isn't about our own importance. 'The friend [best man] who attends the bridegroom waits and listens for him, and is full of joy when he hears the bridegroom's voice. That joy is mine, and it is now complete. He must become greater; I must become less' (3:29–30). We need to be clear that this is by no means a permanent state of affairs, and often Christian service has to be carried through with grim determination and perseverance too. But God, in his goodness, occasionally gives a glimpse of heaven. John 'feels good'. Indeed, there is a note of exhilaration in his voice. But John doesn't feel good because of his status. His joy is triggered and made complete, first by the presence of the bridegroom, and secondly because of the profound sense of contentment that he is in the right place at the right time, serving the purpose for which he was created.

John is 'in his skin', 'in the zone', enjoying an exhilarating sense of 'fit' between desire (to serve the glory of the bridegroom), the opportunity to do so and the possession of the gifts to carry it through. For John 'it just works. It does not draw attention to itself. The toes just work; the ego just works . . . '[10]

Conclusion: above my pay grade?

As we come to the end of this book, you may have noticed that I've illustrated its main teaching points with the lives of three of the great saints of the Bible: Mary, the mother of Jesus, Paul, the apostle to the Gentiles, and John the Baptist, of whom Jesus himself said, 'Among those born of women there [is none] greater' (Matthew 11:11). So you might be forgiven for thinking that finding significance by walking in their steps is way above your pay grade.

You might be forgiven too for a touch of cynicism. The sad reality is that our churches are rife with status anxiety. Even acts of kindness and compassionate service can be motivated by status anxiety. You can spend time listening to other people's problems sympathetically, only because you want to be thought of as a 'good listener' or an 'effective pastor'. In secular work too you can spend hours improving your skills as a competent and effective business manager, not because you care about the godly oversight of God's world, but because you want to be known and admired as a good manager who 'knows his people'. You may even stay behind to tidy up the chairs because you need to maintain your image of 'servant-heartedness'.

Church leaders are especially vulnerable to status anxiety. The sad reality is that, for those who long for attention, approval and admiration, a church fellowship furnishes a ready-made stage, with relatively easy access. Only the other night I listened at length to an older and experienced leader sharing with me how his team apparently 'just keep telling me that all I talk about is Jesus'. This was a man who had just spent twenty-five minutes talking all about himself: 'my' organization, 'my' ideas, 'my' achievements, Me! I wonder whether he senses his craving for recognition and the 'woundedness' that threads its way though his conversation.

I have met senior clergy who seem almost intoxicated with the sound of their own voice. Everyone, it seems, is entitled to hear their opinions. In some churches an unhealthy culture of deference and an obsession with titles and hierarchy can exact a cruel toll on the spiritual formation of leaders. I heard recently how, before processing into a cathedral, bishops could be found anxiously checking with one another for the dates of their consecrations, to make sure that they entered in the correct order. Status anxiety – it's everywhere. And if this is the case with so many of our church leaders, you might wonder what hope there is for the rest of us.

We need to face up to these unpalatable realities and expose them gently to the light of the gospel. But that shouldn't deter us from the hard work of discovering the blessings of godly significance for ourselves. Remember that the moments of self-forgetfulness in the lives of Mary, Paul and John were not likely to have been permanent hallmarks of their personalities either. Paul could be stung and wounded by people's criticism, and I doubt that he was always so successful in repelling the temptation to pride and status-hunger. And John, having waxed so eloquently about the coming of the bridegroom, would soon be sending his disciples to check out his doubts – was Jesus indeed the one, or should they be waiting for another? To quote a cliché, we are all in this together and we shouldn't use the perceived successes and failures of others as an excuse for avoiding our own pilgrimage in spiritual discipleship.

The bigger-than-your-ego trip

So I want to challenge you to join the 'bigger-than-your-ego trip'. As I've said so often in this book, it's going to take time. You will most likely be practising these spiritual disciplines for the rest of your life. Indeed, it's a way of life. Yes, it will be disheartening at times. Like Snakes and Ladders, you will make great strides forwards only to be interrupted by sudden and unpredictable slides backwards. Unravelling neural networks in the brain that have been strengthened through years of practice isn't going to be easy. But it will certainly be worth it.

First, try to *enjoy* practising some of the disciplines. Try to seek out opportunities for feedback rather than dreading it. Be bold, even a little reckless. When you do receive negative feedback, insist to yourself that you are going to see it as an opportunity for developing the art of judging your actions and not judging yourself. Say something like (depending on the situation), 'I may not be a very good teacher in some respects, and I'm deeply disappointed to receive this feedback, but I refuse to judge myself as a person. I refuse to connect my weakness in this specific area of my life with a global judgment about my status and significance as a person.'

If you struggle with voices from the past that say you are hopeless, defective or deficient, try to *enjoy* rebutting them. Insist on telling them that you don't care what they think about you, and you don't even care what you think about you. Be bold, assertive and 'centred' in your determination to tackle these issues. This means, over time, developing a set of thinking tools for different occasions.

One management consultant I know, for example, when arriving at a venue to give a talk, sits for a moment in his car and says, consciously and deliberately, 'I am here to serve the broad purposes of God. To the best of my abilities, I am going to serve God's kingdom by modelling integrity, compassion and diligence. In every encounter I now commit to keeping this priority in mind. I am going to try to fit in, rather than stand out.' Sounds simple? Then try it.

Another person who tends towards competitiveness says, 'God has a piece of work for me to do here. This is one of the "good works" that I was created *for* (Ephesians 2:10). God doesn't want *her* to do it, or *him* to do it. He wants *me* to do it. I'm going to encourage others to chip in with their contributions too, because everything in God's kingdom works better when we pull together for his glory.'

If, like 'Peter' in chapter 9, you have suffered emotional, physical or sexual abuse, then this journey into joy can be slow and hard. You will need to connect with skilled pastoral care or counselling. But it's a journey you have to make, because you can't refuse God's call to experience joy. There will be powerful emotions and much anger. In the early stages you may need to dispute with false and unwanted voices from the past with a great deal of anger and pain. But gradually, over time, if you are determined, God beckons you to a place where you can stand apart from that toxic person or those people and inhabit your place as a loved child of God. The art of disputing with false accusations will be a long, hard road, but, walked steadily, there is the promise that you too will flourish.

Secondly, while refusing to judge yourself before God, don't deprive yourself of the joy of doing something well in his sight. God has called us all to acts of service (including secular employment), and everything we do must be 'as to the Lord'. When it goes well, and especially when other people's feedback coincides with your own 'sober judgment' about the quality of a particular piece of work, don't be afraid to 'feel' God's pleasure in your efforts. Yes, you did it in his strength, using gifts that he gave you – but *you* did it. No more 'It wasn't me; it was the Lord.' Let God love you and take delight in your work!

Thirdly, deal with your acts of sin boldly. Refuse to globalize them in terms of your value and significance as a loved child and servant. I've always been a little nervous about Luther's attempt to jolt us into understanding the radical nature of grace by advising to 'sin boldly', and it's not my intention to attempt an analysis here.[11] But we do need to *deal boldly* with individual acts of sin. As we've seen, guilt and shame are powerful emotions that have the strength to overwhelm our judgment and draw us back into self-condemnation (in the global sense). Be bold, be assertive. Insist that, when you sinned, you sinned as a loved, precious, glorious child of God. That is what makes it so serious and so troublesome. Far from being a licence to sin, maintaining our God-given identity in the face of sin and shame is a motivating force for true repentance. You can't dismiss the seriousness of what you have done, and you have to be ready to shoulder the consequences, but you sinned, repented and now face those consequences as a loved, precious child and servant of God himself, and you must refuse to surrender that identity. Be bold!

Finally, be radically compassionate towards yourself. There's a proper level of respect for your own welfare and your own needs for friendship, fellowship, emotional and physical sustenance, and self-discipline. Again, it's the motivation that counts. We can do these things because we simply want to feel good about ourselves or, from a kingdom perspective, we can care for ourselves because we know that this is how best to serve God's kingdom and add to his glory.

The joy of the zone

Where will it all end? Psychologists talk about a heightened state of loss of self-consciousness called 'flow'.[12] In moments of flow, such as playing a totally enthralling computer game or composing a piece of music, we literally 'lose' ourselves in the work at hand. We are so engaged and absorbed that we don't think about ourselves at all. People who achieve this for a few moments, and occasionally a few hours, describe it as an intensely exhilarating experience.

Have you experienced flow? If not, don't worry, because one day you will. In the words of Charles Wesley's monumental hymn of praise, when heaven breaks in and when we stand before God's throne, we shall 'cast our crowns before him, *lost in wonder love and praise*'.[13] In Eastern religion you are literally lost, absorbed into the great mass of nothingness called 'enlightenment'. In the Christian experience, however, 'flow' comes with a divine trick attached. For we shall also 'rule with him', wielding real power and authority. And then, in a moment of heightened self-forgetfulness in the presence of the bridegroom, we shall discover that we have never felt more like 'ourselves'. It will be a moment of supreme personal significance. It's the bigger-than-your-ego trip. Welcome aboard.

POSTSCRIPT

Back in Seattle, as our overweight telephone salesman 'Stuart' leaves the stage with the applause ringing in his ears, he is about to walk into a trap. People bearing contracts will beat a path to his door, he'll be flooded with invitations to all the smartest events, and – most dangerous of all – friends will begin to laugh at his jokes. His poor ego will receive all the flattery and love that it craves. Until, that is, he gets throat cancer. Or another 'Stuart' shoots to stardom and heaves him to one side. Or his particular style of opera falls out of fashion. Then his ego will deflate like a balloon going pop. Here, ladies and gentleman, it seems we have a loser after all . . .

What would you like to tell Stuart? Wouldn't you want to counsel him not to stake his sense of significance on other people's admiration? Wouldn't you want to say that this is a tough battle for you at times too? Sure enough, he's been blessed with a fabulous voice. But you want to say that those people out there know nothing about him as a person. He needs to keep his value as a singer separate from his value as a person. In fact, we would want to counsel him to drop the language of 'value' and 'worth' altogether. Because Stuart is a Christian, you see, he can understand his sense of identity in a different category altogether: as a loved child of God called to serve God's kingdom. Of course, he is counted as 'worthy' in God's sight, but trying to drum up 'feelings of worth' risks driving him back into making the same old comparisons and trying to stand out. So we'll tell him simply to stop trying to 'value' and boost his self-worth altogether. Instead, we'll say, it's healthier to think in terms of showing yourself compassion.

In fact, we'll want to tell Stuart much more about radical, biblical self-compassion. We'll tell him that it means a commitment to dispute with those 'no-good' feelings and thoughts that have undermined his confidence for so many years. Stuart can learn to enjoy his gift of singing, and his other strengths too, as gifts from God, rather than allowing them to define him as a person. And self-compassion offers him the tools to dispute with the negative voices from his father whose expectations he will never meet.

When Stuart messes up, we'll tell him that he needs to dispute with thoughts of self-condemnation and self-hatred. 'When you fail at something, go easy on yourself, Stuart. Life is hard. Other people fail too. God is patient and kind. Keep your eye on the big picture, pick yourself up and get back to working for him. Do you love your son? Sure you do. Then remember that God loves you as his own Son, with the same fervour and passion. But Stuart, when you sin, take it seriously. Your conscience is alerting you to the seriousness of this and the possible consequences you face. You need to come to him in confession. And you may need to put into place accountability with another Christian to help you avoid this sin again.'

'But Stuart, don't ever, EVER let messing up strip you of your identity as God's loved son and plunge you back into self-condemnation. Because you did a bad thing, remember, that no longer defines you as a "bad" person. Be bold. Be resolute. Refuse to condemn yourself.'

As we leave Stuart and head to London, the kids are still chanting, 'It's good to be me; it's good to be me.' Maybe somebody needs to tell them to stop. But seriously, do we really want our kids to grow up chanting, 'Believe in yourself', absorbed with being 'special'? What happens when everybody thinks they are special? What happens when *everybody* has been overpraised throughout childhood to believe they are future *X Factor* contestants? A lot of disappointment.

So if your kids' teachers are being seduced with too much self-esteem ideology, why not pop down to the school and request a quiet chat? It's a matter of perspective. Some kids need to hear these positive messages, as a corrective to the harsh messages coming from home. But you might suggest that you want your child to know that they are unique, rather than special. They are special to you, hugely loved and valued by you, yes. But out there in the big, wide world, better unique than special. 'Special' is uniqueness with the dangerous added ingredient of importance, perhaps even greatness. Do you really want to condemn your child to that particular treadmill? Many schools are already responding to these concerns and beginning to substitute resilience programmes for self-esteem. Let's encourage that.

And then, in the modern world, with its emphasis on teamwork and co-operation, do you want your kids to be so conscious of difference? Rather than focusing on how different they are, how they stand out and how they can be distinguished from others, why not suggest that teachers ensure a balance by teaching the importance of things we have in common: fitting in rather than standing out? And at home, how much do you set the tone for a compassionate, outward-looking mindset in the way you conduct relationships? Is your home-life alive with values of compassion, looking out for one another and finding ways of chipping in? Or is there an undercurrent of criticism and condemnation running through the family?

Should we discourage competition? Not at all. Competing is a means of getting the best out of yourself and a great way to benchmark your skills. What matters is how we *interpret* winning and losing. Competition is also a great way to teach our kids how to fail well. Failing well is one of life's most crucial skills, but it's rarely taught well. So here's an original idea. Get the kids to play a new game called 'pass the parcel'. But make sure there is only one prize in the middle of all those layers of wrapping. Ask the kids to cheer when the music stops and the paper gets ripped off and there's still nothing there. Hey, life's like that! You win some and you lose some.

Finally, remember to praise effort rather than status. Kids need to hear phrases like, 'Hey, hardly anybody gets things right first time. But I like the way you tried. Let's figure out together how we can get this to work.' Don't overpraise. We want our kids to be resilient, with inherent 'bounce-back', prepared as well as they can be to cope with life's tough adversities and disappointments. And rather than worrying about how they are feeling right now, we want them to be hungry learners, eager to make a difference in the world, confident that they have something (along with all the others) to offer in compassionate service to others.

Most of all, we want them to grow up in the gospel. They are not the centre of the world, and we shouldn't be treating them as though they are. As they gradually become aware of wrongdoing, we shouldn't duck our responsibility to help them see that sinful acts are wrong, that sin destroys and needs forgiveness. And they need to know that they are loved.

Loved by their Maker as unique, wonderful and full of potential for serving him and others.

Back in the United States, let's return to that small church hall in the Midwest where a young mother is calling her Sunday school lesson to order. The wall poster is still there, and the fair-skinned Jesus still smiles benignly at the happy group of Western children gathered around his knee. 'You're special!' he is telling them.

But somebody has got hold of a large red felt pen and has inserted five extra words in large letters. It now reads, 'You're **part of something** special. **Follow me!**'

NOTES

Introduction

1. There are a number of quotes from Donald Trump at MoneyWeek online: http://www. moneyweek.com/news-and-charts/profile-donald-trump (accessed 29 September 2012).

2. The term was first coined by the psychologist Martin Seligman (see ch. 8, pp. 125–126).

3. Michael Foley, *The Age of Absurdity: Why Modern Life Makes It Hard to Be Happy* (Simon & Schuster, 2010), p. 64.

1. Birth of an ideology

1. Jonny Wilkinson, *Tackling Life* (Headline, 2008).

2. William James (1890), *The Principles of Psychology* (repr. Harvard University Press, 1983).

3. Or more strictly, the 'father of American psychology', because it was the German physiologist Wilhelm Wundt who first applied experimental principles to the study of mental processes, in a book published in 1874.

4. For an excellent biographical overview, see Robert D. Richardson, *William James: In the Maelstrom of American Modernism* (Houghton Mifflin Harcourt, 2006).

5. Sigmund Freud (1920), 'Beyond the Pleasure Principle', in James Strachey (ed.), *The Standard Edition of the Complete Psychological Works of Sigmund Freud* (Hogarth Press and The Institute of Psychoanalysis, 1953–1974).

6. Sigmund Freud, *New Introductory Lectures on Psychoanalysis* (Penguin Freud Library 2, 1933), pp. 105–106.

7. Alfred Adler, *The Science of Living* (Doubleday, 1969).

8. Jack L. Rubins, *Karen Horney: Gentle Rebel of Psychoanalysis* (Summit Books, 1978).

9. Karen Horney, *Our Inner Conflicts* (W. W. Norton, 1945), p. 41.

10. Ibid., p. 219.

11. John Bowlby, *Maternal Care and Mental Health* (The World Health Organization, 1951).

12. M. Ainsworth, M. Blehar, E. Waters and S. Wall, *Patterns of Attachment* (Erlbaum, 1978).

13. I. Bretherton, 'The Origins of Attachment Theory: John Bowlby and Mary Ainsworth', *Developmental Psychology* 28 (1992).

2. Tipping point

1. Morton M. Grodzins, *The Metropolitan Area as a Racial Problem* (University of Pittsburgh Press, 1958).

2. Malcolm Gladwell, *The Tipping Point: How Little Things Can Make a Big Difference* (Little Brown, 2000), p. 12.

3. Steven Ward, 'Filling the World with Self-Esteem: A Social History of Truth-Making', *Canadian Journal of Sociology* 21 (1996).

4. B. L. Beyerstein, 'Whence Cometh the Myth that We Only Use 10% of Our Brains?', in S. Della Sala, *Mind Myths: Exploring Everyday Mysteries of the Mind and Brain* (John Wiley, 1999).

5. I am grateful to Christopher J. Mruk for this analogy: Christopher J. Mruk, *Self-Esteem Research, Theory and Practice* (Springer Publishing Company, 2006), p. 18.

6. J. M. Twenge and W. K. Campbell, *The Narcissism Epidemic* (Free Press, 2009), p. 64.

7. F. Rodewalt and M. W. Tragakis, 'Self-Esteem and Self-regulation', *Psychological Inquiry* 14 (2003), p. 1.

8. M. Rosenberg, *Society and the Adolescent Self-Image* (Princeton University Press, 1965).

9. Ibid., pp. 17–18.

10. http://www.wwnorton.com/college/psych/psychsci/media/rosenberg.htm.

11. For an authoritative review, see N. Emler, *Self-Esteem: The Costs and Causes of Low Self-Worth* (Joseph Rowntree Foundation, 2001).

12. For a comprehensive overview, see Howard Kirschenbaum and Valerie L. Henderson (eds.), *The Carl Rogers Reader* (Houghton Mifflin, 1989).

13. Carl Rogers, *On Becoming a Person* (Houghton Miffin, 1961), p. 37.

14. Paul C. Vitz, *Psychology as Religion: The Cult of Self-Worship* (Lion Publishing, 1979), p. 48.

15. Steve Gillon, *Boomer Nation: The Largest and Richest Generation Ever, and How It Changed America* (Free Press, 2004), Introduction, p. 5.

16. Eugène Delacroix, *The Journal of Eugene Delacroix*, trans. W. Patch (Convici-Friede, 1937), p. 93.

3. Catch them young and sell it hard

1. A. Revel, 'How to Marry Yourself', http://www.loveromancerelationship.com/how-to-marry-yourself/ (accessed 2 July 2011).

2. http://www.self-esteem-nase.org.

3. http://www.self-esteem-nase.org/.

4. http://www.self-esteem-nase.org/products.php (accessed 30 September 2012).

5. http://www.self-esteem-nase.org/booster.php (accessed 30 September 2012).

6. *California Task Force to Promote Self-Esteem and Personal and Social Responsibility* (California State Department of Education, 1990).

7. http://pops.com/ (accessed 16 June 2012).

8. http://drwilliammitchell.com/ (accessed 16 June 2012).

9. The promotional material of POPS focuses on the importance of positive achievement and a healthy school atmosphere, rather than delving too much into the 'deep' causes of low self-esteem. Thus, 'Children must experience success in order to develop and sustain a positive self-concept.' The POPS programme basically has two core messages. First, because self-esteem is learned, it can be taught; the educational challenge is to teach and enable students to like themselves. But secondly, because of the link between self-concept and achievement, schools must develop a positive climate that creates opportunities for all children to develop a sense of growth and accomplishment in the classroom and outside. So in the POPS philosophy, a broadly-based positive learning climate that includes school, home and community is crucial. But it is also worth noting that, according to this philosophy, self-esteem isn't simply a prize you award yourself; it is something that is developed through real-life achievement too.

10. P. Renshaw, 'Self-Esteem Research and Equity Programmes for Girls: A Reassessment', in J. Kenway and S. Willis (eds.), *Hearts and Minds: Self-Esteem and the Schooling of Girls* (Falmer Press, 1990).

11. J. Kenway and S. Willis (eds.), *Hearts and Minds: Self-Esteem and the Schooling of Girls* (Falmer Press, 1990), pp. 1–13.

12. Ibid., p. 7.

13. M. Borba and C. Borba, *Self-Esteem: A Classroom Affair – 101 Ways to Help Children Like Themselves* (Winston Press, 1982).

14. https://www.education.gov.uk/publications/ eOrderingDownload/DFE-RR049.pdf (accessed 5 November 2012).

15. Patrick West, *Conspicuous Compassion: Why Sometimes It Really Is Cruel to Be Kind* (Civitas, 2004), p. 11.

16. Alexandra Robbins, *Conquering Your Quarterlife Crisis* (Perigee, 2004), p. 52.

17. http://www.mtv.com/news/articles/1493464/britney-posthoneymoon-posts-another-letter.jhtml?headlines=true (accessed 1 October 2012).

18. Alexandra Gill, http://www.theglobeandmail.com/life/ food-and-wine/article174455.ece (accessed 30 May 2012).

19. Tania Branigan, 'Key to the Good Life: Looking after Your Own Interests', at http://www.guardian.co.uk/uk/2006/jul/ 04/internationalaidanddevelopment.g8 (accessed 30 June 2012).

20. The Henley Centre, 'The Responsibility Gap' (Salvation Army Publications, 2004), p. 27.

21. 'Not All the Young Are Selfish', *Washington Post*, 1987: http:// www.highbeam.com/doc/1P2-1328316.html (accessed 5 November 2012).

22. J. M. Twenge, *Generation Me* (Simon & Schuster, 2006), p. 13.

23. J. M. Twenge and W. K. Campbell, 'Age and Birth Cohort Differences in Self-Esteem: A Cross-Temporal Meta-Analysis', *Personality and Social Psychology Review* 5 (2001), pp. 321–344.

24. R. Hicks and K. Hicks, *Boomers, X-ers, and Other Strangers* (Tyndale, 1999), p. 270.

25. C. R. Newsom *et al.*, 'Changes in Adolescent Response Patterns on the MMPI across 4 Decades', *Journal of Personality Assessment* 81 (2003), pp. 78–84.

26. Twenge, *Generation Me*, title page.

4. To God you're big stuff!

1. Tanya Luhrmann, *When God Talks Back: Understanding the American Evangelical Relationship with God* (Alfred A. Knopf, 2012), p. 72.

2. D. Capps, 'Narcissism and the Changing Face of Conversion', *Journal of Religion and Health* 29:3 (1990), p. 248.

3. Brian M. Howard, 'The Butterfly Song' (Copyright: Mission Hills Music).

4. From 'Once in Royal David's City'.

5. Luhrmann, *When God Talks Back*, p. 15.

6. Ibid., p. 20.

7. Ibid., p. 19.

8. Stephen R. Prothero, *American Jesus: How the Son of God Became a National Icon* (Farrar, Straus and Giroux, 2003), p. 127.

9. Luhrmann, *When God Talks Back,* pp. 21–23.

10. Ibid., p. 72.

11. Kay M. Strom, *Perfect in His Eyes: A Woman's Workshop on Self-Esteem* (Zondervan, 1988).

12. Renee C. Cobb, *10 Steps to Revolutionize Your Life* (Make A Difference Publishing, 1996).

13. Max Lucado, *You Are Special* (Lion Hudson, 2004).

14. Max Lucado, *Best of All* (Lion Hudson, 2003).

15. Walter Trobisch, *Love Yourself: Self-Acceptance and Depression* (Inter-Varsity Press, 1976), p. 11.

16. The Barna group have interesting research data on teenagers' attitudes to church going, available at: http://www.barna.org/teens-next-gen-articles/93-what-teenagers-look-for-in-a-church (accessed 30 May 2012).

17. Wade Clark Roof, quoted in D. A. Roozen and C. K. Hadaway (eds.), *Church and Denominational Growth* (Abingdon Press, 1993), p. 265.

18. J. M. Twenge and W. K. Campbell, *The Narcissism Epidemic* (Free Press, 2009), p. 246.

19. Ibid., p. 248.

20. Ibid., p. 249.

21. Ibid., p. 248.

22. Ibid.

23. G. A. Pritchard, *Willow Creek Seeker Services* (Baker Books, 1996), p. 234.

5. Does boosterism work?

1. http://depression.about.com/cs/teenchild/a/teensex.htm.

2. R. F. Baumeister, J. D. Campbell, J. I. Krueger and K. D. Vohs, 'Does High Self-Esteem Cause Better Performance, Interpersonal Success, Happiness, or Healthier Lifestyles?', *Psychological Science in the Public Interest* 4:1 (2003), pp. 1–44.

3. N. Elmer, *Self-Esteem: The Costs and Causes of Low Self-Worth* (Joseph Rowntree Foundation, 2001).

4. R. F. Baumeister, 'Violent Pride', *Scientific American* 284:4 (2001), pp. 96–101.

5. Baumeister, Campbell, Krueger and Vohs, 'Does High Self-Esteem Cause Better Performance, Interpersonal Success, Happiness, or Healthier Lifestyles?', p. 7.

6. Ibid., p. 8.

7. J. Bishop and H. Inderbitzen, 'Peer Acceptance and Friendship: An Investigation', *Journal of Early Adolescence* 15 (1995), pp. 476–489.

8. C. E. Rusbult, G. D. Morrow and D. J. Johnson, 'Self-Esteem and Problem Solving Behaviour in Close Relationships', *British Journal of Social Psychology* 26 (1987), pp. 293–303.

9. C. Paul, J. Fitzjohn, P. Herbison and N. Dickson, 'The Determinants of Sexual Intercourse before Age 16', *Journal of Adolescent Health* 27 (2000), pp. 136–147.

10. J. M. Boden and L. J. Horwood, 'Self-Esteem, Risky Sexual Behaviour, and Pregnancy in a New Zealand Birth Cohort', *Archives of Sexual Behaviour* 35 (2006), pp. 549–560.

11. Emler, *Self-Esteem*.

12. L. Yablonsky, *Gangsters: Fifty Years of Madness, Drugs, and Death on the Streets of America* (NYU Press, 1998), p. 79.

13. M. B. Donnellan, K. H. Trzesniewski, R. W. Robins, T. E. Moffitt and A. Caspi, 'Low Self-Esteem Is Related to Aggression, Antisocial Behavior, and Delinquency', *Psychological Science* 16(4) (April 2005), pp. 328–335.

14. K. H. Trzesniewski, M. B. Donnellan, T. E. Moffitt, R. W. Robins, R. Poulton and A. Caspi, 'Low Self-Esteem During Adolescence Predicts Poor Health, Criminal Behavior, and Limited Economic Prospects During Adulthood', *Developmental Psychology* 42 (2006), pp. 381–390.

15. B. J. Bushman and R. F. Baumeister, 'Threatened Egotism, Narcissism, Self-Esteem, and Direct and Displaced Aggression: Does Self-Love or Self-Hate Lead to Violence?', *Journal of Personality and Social Psychology* 75, (1998), pp. 219–229.

16. Baumeister, Campbell, Krueger and Vohs, 'Does High Self-Esteem Cause Better Performance, Interpersonal Success, Happiness, or Healthier Lifestyles?', p. 21.

17. California Task Force to Promote Self-Esteem and Personal and Social Responsibility, *Toward a State of Self-Esteem* (California State Department of Education, 1990).

18. N. J. Smelser, 'Self-Esteem and Social Problems: An Introduction', in A. M. Mecca, N. J. Smelser and J. Vasconcellos (eds.), *The Social Importance of Self-Esteem* (University of California Press, 1989), pp. 15–17.

6. The age of the narcissist

1. J. V. Wood, E. Perunovic and J. W. Lee, 'Positive Self-Statements: Power for Some, Peril for Others', *Psychological Science* 3 (2009), pp. 1–7.

2. R. J. Sternberg, quoted in G. Matthews, M. Zeidner and R. Roberts, *Emotional Intelligence: Science and Myth* (Bradford Books, 2003), from the Foreword, p. xii.

3. P. Barnes, E. Powell-Griner, K. McFann and R. Nahin, 'Complementary and Alternative Medicine Use among Adults: United States 2002', *CDC Advance Data Report* 343 (May 2004).

4. Alissa Lim, Noel Cranswick and Michael South, 'Adverse Events Associated with the Use of Complementary and Alternative Medicine in Children', *Archives of Disease in Childhood* 96:3 (2011), pp. 297–300.

5. Sternberg, in *Emotional Intelligence: Science and Myth*, from the Foreword, p. xii.

6. Wood, Perunovic and Lee, 'Positive Self-Statements', pp. 860–866.

7. M. P. Zanna, 'Message Receptivity: A New Look at the Old Problem of Open- Versus Closed-Mindedness', in A. Mitchell (ed.), *Advertising Exposure, Memory and Choice* (Erbaum, 1993), pp. 141–162.

8. http://www.youtube.com/watch?v=rm9jBH7ufRU (accessed 3 July 2011).

9. http://www.youtube.com/watch?v=yqVOIWgtu50&NR=1 (accessed 3 July 2011).

10. http://www.uwyo.edu/lrn/resources/genme.asp (accessed 3 July 2011).

11. See C. Lasch, *The Culture of Narcissism: American Life in an Age of Diminishing Expectations* (Norton, 1979).

12. J. M. Twenge, *Generation Me* (Simon & Schuster, 2006).

13. Twenge, *Generation Me,* pp. 68–71.

14. C. R. Newsom *et al.*, 'Changes in Adolescent Response Patterns on the MMPI Across Four Decades', *Journal of Personality Assessment* 81 (2003), pp. 78–84.

15. L. Katz and M. Stout, *The Feel-Good Curriculum* (Perseus Books, 2000).

16. This whole area is discussed extensively in J. M. Twenge and W. K. Campbell, *The Narcissism Epidemic* (Free Press, 2009), pp. 195–210.

17. B. M. Bushman and R. F. Baumeister, 'Threatened Egotism, Narcissism, Self-Esteem, and Direct and Displaced Aggression: Does Self-Love or Self-Hate Lead to Violence?', *Journal of Personality and Social Psychology* 75 (1998), pp. 219–229.

18. *The Prince's Trust YouGov Youth Index 2008*, The Prince's Trust, London, UK.

19. For example, P. J. Wickramaratne *et al.*, 'Age, Period, and Cohort Effects on the Risk of Major Depression: Results from Five United States Communities', *Journal of Clinical Epidemiology* 42:4 (1989), pp. 333–343.

20. A study, among the largest of its kind, carried out by Columbia University in New York in 2004 illustrates how dangerous it can be to assume that changes in rates of mental disorders are focused in a particular generation (such as Twenge's 'generation Me' born after 1970): Deborah S. Hasin, Renee D. Goodwin, Frederick S. Stinson and Bridget F. Grant, 'Epidemiology of Major Depressive Disorder', *Archives of General Psychiatry* 62: 1097–1106 (2005). Around 5% of US adults had experienced a Major Depressive Disorder (a mental illness) in the twelve months preceding the survey. But in previous surveys conducted during the 1980s and 1990s it was the younger adult population that seemed to be most at risk; in contrast, by 2004 late middle-aged adults seemed to have the highest risk. The authors concluded, 'This marks an important transformation in the distribution of Major Depressive Disorder in the general population and a specific risk for baby-boomers aged 45 to 64 years.' In other words, the highest risk was now among those born before the generation Me period of 1970–1990.

21. For an example of research that has highlighted the pitfalls of these comparisons, see http://www.ncbi.nlm.nih.gov/pubmed/7636512?ordinalpos=1&itool=EntrezSystem2.PEntrez.Pubmed.Pubmed_ResultsPanel.Pubmed_DiscoveryPanel.Pubmed_RVAbstractPlus, and http://www.ncbi.nlm.nih.gov/pubmed/1309177?ordinalpos=1&itool=EntrezSystem2.PEntrez.Pubmed.Pubmed_ResultsPanel.Pubmed_DiscoveryPanel.Pubmed_Discovery_RA&linkpos=1&logs=relatedarticles&logdbfrom=pubmed.

22. Neil Howe and William Strauss, *Millennials Rising: The Next Generation* (Vintage, 2000), pp. 3–120.

7. Kids praise

1. K. Ecclestone and D. Hayes, *The Dangerous Rise of Therapeutic Education* (Routledge, 2009), p. 164.

2. N. Emler, *Self-Esteem: The Costs and Causes of Low Self-Worth* (Joseph Rowntree Foundation, 2001), p. 3.

3. J. M. Twenge and W. K. Campbell, *The Narcissism Epidemic* (Free Press, 2009), p. 74.

4. Ibid., p. 75.

5. http://www.centreforconfidence.co.uk/docs/SEALsummary.pdf.

6. Ecclestone and Hayes, *The Dangerous Rise of Therapeutic Education*, p. 164.

7. http://ebmh.bmj.com/content/1/4/118.full.

8. '[The self-esteem movement] argued that raising self-esteem was a panacea which would cure all social ills. Subsequent evidence has not supported this and has shown that self-esteem is not important for academic achievement . . . social problems (such as bullying, violence or antisocial behaviour) often occur as a result of people who have high, not low, self-esteem. Despite the lack of robust supporting evidence, the self-esteem movement was successful in creating a bandwagon

which led to distinct child rearing and educational practices. One was to put a great deal of emphasis on helping to make the children feel good about him/herself. This led to unwarranted praise, restriction of competition and criticism, and aspirational grading. It also led to an emphasis on "all about me / I'm special activities" and a focus on feeling and emotions.' http://www.centreforconfidence.co.uk/docs/SEALsummary.pdf, p. 7.

9. C. K. West, J. A. Fish and J. Stevens, 'General Self-Concept, Self-Concept of Academic Ability and School Achievement: Implications for Causes of Self-Concept', *American Journal of Education* 24 (1980), pp. 194–213.

10. L. Feinstein, 'The Relative Economic Importance of Academic, Psychological and Behavioural Attributes Developed in Childhood', Unpublished paper (Centre for Economic Performance, London School of Economics, 2000).

11. M. Phillips, *All Must Have Prizes* (Sphere, 1997).

12. Carol S. Dweck, *The Perils and Promises of Praise* (Educational Leadership, 2007).

13. Explored at length in Carol S. Dweck, *Mindset: How You Can Fulfil Your Potential* (Robinson Publishing, 2012).

14. A. D. Nussbaum and C. S. Dweck, 'Defensiveness vs. Remediation: Self-Theories and Modes of Self-Esteem Maintenance', *Personality and Social Psychology Bulletin* 34 (2008), pp. 599–612.

15. Carol Dweck's book *Mindset: How You Can Fulfil Your Potential* is full of similar practical advice.

16. Emler, *Self-Esteem: The Costs and Causes of Low Self-Worth*, p. 44.

8. All roads lead to philosophy

1. This illustration was inspired by a similar one presented in Christopher J. Mruk, *Self-Esteem Research, Theory and Practice* (Springer Publishing, 2006), p. 8.

2. The term has sometimes been used in legal cases. For example, in one case the judge referred to 'the well-known elephant test. It is difficult to describe, but you know it when you see it.' Cadogan Estates Ltd v Morris; EWCA Civ 1671 (4 November 1998) (at paragraph 17) [Author: I must confess, though, I can't see why an elephant is more difficult to describe than anything else!].

3. N. Branden, *The Power of Self-Esteem* (Health Communications, 1992), p. xii.

4. http://blog.nathanielbranden.com/2008-04/the-importance-of-definitions/ (accessed 5 November 2012).

5. Mruk, *Self-Esteem Research, Theory and Practice*, p. 9.

6. David Hume, *A Treatise of Human Nature*, 2nd edn, text revised by P. G. Nidditch (Oxford University Press, 1978), p. 252.

7. I am indebted to Julian Baggini's brilliant exploration of the 'pearl' versus 'bundle' theories of self in his book, J. Baggini, *The Ego Trick: What Does It Mean to Be You* (Granta Publications, 2011), pp. 119–121.

8. Paul C. Vitz, *Psychology as Religion: The Cult of Self-Worship* (Lion Publishing, 1979), p. 48.

9. B. F. Skinner made this and similar points in his classic debate with Carl Rogers: B. F. Skinner and C. Rogers, *Some Issues Concerning the Control of Human Behaviour* (Amazon Digital Services, 2011 Kindle edn).

10. A. Ellis, *The Myth of Self-Esteem: How Rational Emotive Therapy Can Change Your Life* (Prometheus Books, 2005), p. 37.

11. Ibid., p. 38.

12. R. S. Hartman, http://www.strandtheory.org/images/Hartman_-_The_individual_in_management.pdf (accessed 20 December 2012).

13. Ellis, *The Myth of Self-Esteem: How Rational Emotive Therapy Can Change Your Life*, p. 44.

14. Ibid., p. 83.

15. M. Seligman, *Authentic Happiness: Using the New Positive Psychology to Realize Your Potential for Lasting Fulfilment* (Free Press, 2002).

16. M. Seligman, *The Optimistic Child* (Houghton Mifflin, 1995), p. 50.

17. J. Crocker, M. Olivier and N. Nuer, 'Self-Image Goals and Compassionate Goals: Costs and Benefits', *Self and Identity* 8:2–3 (2009), pp. 251–269.

18. J. Crocker and L. E. Park, 'The Costly Pursuit of Self-Esteem', *Psychological Bulletin* 130 (2004), pp. 392–414.

19. Ibid., p. 406.

20. J. Crocker and N. Nuer, 'Do People Need Self-Esteem?' *Psychological Bulletin* 130: 3 (2004), pp. 469–472.

21. Augustine of Hippo, *Confessions*, ch. 1.

9. We did it my way

1. E. Becker, *The Birth and Death of Meaning*, 2nd edn (Free Press, 1971), p. 33.

2. This is a theologically contentious area. However, I am persuaded by the work of Reformed scholars, who argue that man's condition was not meant to be static, and that Adam's nature had potential for growth and maturity. Thus Berkhof explains, 'This does not mean that [Adam] had already reached the highest state of excellence of which he was capable, he was destined to reach a higher degree of perfection through obedience . . . His condition was a preliminary or temporary one, which would either lead on to greater perfection and glory or terminate in the fall.' L. Berkhof, *Systematic Theology* (Eerdmans, 1996). Similarly Calvin: 'Truly the first man would have passed to a better life, had he remained upright.' J. Calvin, *Commentary on Genesis* (Banner of Truth Trust, 1965). This doesn't mean that man was not perfect as originally made. But, like a part-inflated

balloon is a perfect example of what it is at that point, this does not preclude a greater perfection as it is inflated to its full potential.

3. M. Horton, *The Christian Faith: A Systematic Theology for Pilgrims on the Way* (Zondervan, 2011), p. 386.

4. John Gray, *Straw Gods: Thoughts on Humans and Other Animals* (Granta Publications, 2002), p. 28.

5. Ibid., p. 28.

6. Ibid., p. 17.

7. M. Alicke and C. Sedikides, 'Self-Enhancement and Self-Protection: What They Are and What They Do', *European Review of Social Psychology* 20 (2009), pp. 1–48.

8. Justin Kruger and David Dunning, 'Unskilled and Unaware of It: How Difficulties in Recognizing One's Own Incompetence Lead to Inflated Self-Assessments', *Journal of Personality and Social Psychology* 77:6 (1999), pp. 1121–1134.

9. David G. Myers, *Exploring Social Psychology* (McGraw-Hill, 1994), pp. 15–19.

10. E. Becker, *The Denial of Death* (Free Press, 1973), p. 26.

11. For example, J. Greenberg, T. Pyszczynski and S. Solomon, 'The Causes and Consequences of a Need for Self-Esteem: A Terror Management Theory', in R. F. Baumeister (ed.), *Public Self and Private Self* (Springer-Verlag, 1986), pp. 189–212.

12. T. Pyszczynski *et al.*, 'Why Do People Need Self-Esteem? A Theoretical and Empirical Review', *Psychological Bulletin* 130 (2004), pp. 435–467.

13. For a full and scholarly analysis of psychological thinking about the emotion of shame, see G. Kaufman, *The Psychology of Shame*, 2nd edn (Springer Publishing, 1996).

14. For a detailed overview of the relationship between pride and low self-esteem, see T. Cooper, *Sin, Pride and Self-Acceptance* (Inter-Varsity Press, 2003).

15. C. Ash, *Pure Joy: Rediscover Your Conscience* (Inter-Varsity Press, 2012), ch. 5.

16. J. R. W. Stott, *The Message of 2 Timothy*, Bible Speaks Today (Inter-Varsity Press, 1999), pp. 19–20.

10. Amazed by grace

1. http://www.self-esteem-nase.org/ (accessed 3 September 2012).

2. H. Norman Wright, *Improving Your Self Image* (Harvest House, 1977), p. 8.

3. Dick Keyes, *Beyond Identity* (Servant Books, 1984), p. 90.

4. Ibid.

5. Quoted by Keyes, *Beyond Identity*, p. 90.

6. For a full analysis of the Greek text, see I. H. Marshall, *The Gospel of Luke: A Commentary on the Greek Text* (Paternoster Press, 1978).

7. Ibid.

8. Keyes, *Beyond Identity*, p. 76.

9. Timothy Keller, *The Freedom of Self-Forgetfulness* (10Publishing, 2012), p. 25.

10. Ibid.

11. C. S. Lewis, *Mere Christianity* (Fontana Books, 1961), p. 178.

12. One of the most popular exponents of self-compassion within a secular worldview is Kristin Neff: http://www.self-compassion.org/self-compassion-the-book/about-the-book.html (accessed 1 October 2012).

13. Ibid.

11. How to stop judging yourself

1. http://www.youtube.com/watch?v=BYLMTvxOaeE.

2. U. Herwig, K. Kaffenberger, T. Baumgartner and L. Jancke, 'Neural Correlates of a "Pessimistic" Attitude When

Anticipating Events of Unknown Emotional Valence', *NeuroImage* 34 (2007), pp. 848–858.

3. Hans J. Hillerbrand, *The Division of Christendom: Christianity in the Sixteenth Century* (John Knox Press, 2007).

4. M. Seligman, *The Optimistic Child* (Houghton Mifflin, 1995), p. 194.

5. Timothy Keller, *The Freedom of Self-Forgetfulness* (10Publishing, 2012), p. 33.

12. The bigger-than-your-ego trip!

1. George M. Foster, 'Peasant Society and the Image of Limited Good', *American Anthropologist* 67 (1965), pp. 293–315.

2. I am grateful to Jerome H. Neyrey and Richard L. Rohrbaugh for their insights into this area. See 'He Must Increase, I Must Decrease (John 3:30): A Social and Cultural Interpretation': http://www.nd.edu/~jneyrey1/LimitedGoods.html.

3. Foster, 'Peasant Society and the Image of Limited Good', p. 296.

4. Alain de Botton, *Status Anxiety* (Penguin Books, 2005), p. vii. De Botton's work is a comprehensive and thoughtful introduction to the whole area of status anxiety.

5. Adam Smith, *The Theory of Moral Sentiments* (1759), http://knarf.english.upenn.edu/Smith/tms132.html.

6. De Botton, *Status Anxiety*, p. 15.

7. Plutarch, *Moralia*, vol. 1 (Loeb Classical Library), p. 237.

8. De Botton, *Status Anxiety*, p. 46.

9. D. A. Carson, *The Gospel According to John* (Apollos, 1991), p. 211.

10. Timothy Keller, *The Freedom of Self-Forgetfulness* (10Publishing, 2012), p. 33.

11. A scholarly and detailed analysis of Luther's meaning, including full referencing by J. Swan (2005), can be downloaded at http://tquid.sharpens.org/sin_boldly.htm#_edn23. (accessed 30 September 2012).

12. The concept of 'flow' is connected mostly with a psychologist called Mihaly Csikszentmihalyi. He has written several books in this area, including M. Csikszentmihalyi, *Flow: The Psychology of Optimal Experience*, 1st edn (Harper Perennial Modern Classics, 2008).

13. Charles Wesley, 'Love Divine, All Loves Excelling' (1747).

Inter-Varsity Press

For more information about IVP
and our publications visit
www.ivpbooks.com

Get regular updates at **ivpbooks.com/signup**
Find us on **facebook.com/ivpbooks**
Follow us on **twitter.com/ivpbookcentre**

Inter-Varsity Press, a company limited by guarantee registered in England and Wales, number 05202650. Registered
office IVP Bookcentre, Norton Street, Nottingham NG7 3HR, United Kingdom. Registered charity number 1105757.